A NEW ENGLISH GRAMMAR

- American Edition

Andrew Rossiter

Linguapress

ISBN-13: 979 - 1069977631
International English edition first published 2020 under the title
A Descriptive Grammar of English.
American edition first published 2021.
Revision 2.0.1. 2024

Imprint - Linguapress. Website – Linguapress.com

This book is also available in French
 Nouvelle grammaire descriptive de l'anglais. ISBN 979 - 8650107736

Reviews of this American English edition

"A New English Grammar Has All the Answers
   This book is one of the most practical grammar reference books we've seen, where each grammar point is explained in a very simple way with helpful examples as well as warnings about usage pitfalls in only 200 pages of nice, clear, easy-to-read print.....
   A New English Grammar – American Edition by Andrew Rossiter is a very useful resource for teachers and learners alike, and we appreciate the clarity, organization, and ease of use. We both feel that it would be a valuable addition to any teacher's collection.
   WAESOL Educator Washington Summer 2022

"This concise and useful reference book …. will make for a significant and appreciated companion to the majority of ESL textbooks or American English grammar books for students involved in the complexities of learning English as their second, third or fourth language ."
   CATESOL Blog – California , 2022

"(This book) is appropriate for students with elementary to upper-intermediate levels of English proficiency. The use of different font colors to emphasize key words in the text is another advantage of this ... valuable resource for both learners and teachers of English as a Second or Foreign Language. This book can be either self-studied or taught by teachers, ... and covers all the grammatical topics needed for teachers in an English class."
   Currents magazine – from MATSOL, Massachusetts, 2022

Reviews of the original international English version of this book:

   "Overall, this is a useful reference book to have on hand when planning for and teaching grammar lessons. The clarity of explanations and wealth of examples, alongside helpful visual keys, provide both new and experienced teachers with something easy to dip into, regardless of the language level they are teaching."
   EFL Magazine – 2021

Preface

A New English Grammar

Introduction to the American English edition

A New English Grammar was originally published under the title *A Descriptive Grammar of English* as an international English edition describing the grammar of British English. This new edition prioritizes American English in the rare cases where it differs from British English. Ideal for teachers and students, it covers all the fundamental points of grammar that need to be mastered for the preparation of SATs and for the development of essential English writing skills.

Is it necessary to have a special American English edition? To be quite honest, the answer is "not really", though American readers and international students wanting specifically to learn American English will find it useful! It is important to stress, however, that British English and American English are **one and the same language,** and as far as grammar is concerned, there are actually *very* few differences between the English of the United States and the English of England. By far the biggest and most easily recognizable difference between American and British forms of English only affects the spoken language, since it a question of accent, or phonetics. British and American accents are clearly different.

As far as the written language is concerned, the most visible differences between American and British English concern **vocabulary** and **spelling**, not **grammar**; but even then, while these involve some very common words, they are not particularly frequent. Common American words like *faucet sidewalk* and *diapers* are almost unknown in Britain (where people say *tap pavement* and *nappies*); but these are exceptions to the general rule, which is that we use **the same** words with **the same** meanings on either side of the Atlantic.

As for spelling, generally speaking words are written the same way too.... with a few variations. Americans write a lot of verbs ending in *-ize*, while people in Britain will write them ending in *-ise or -ize*. Americans write *color, humor* and *labor,* while people in Britain write *colour, humour* and *labour.* But many readers are familiar with both spellings in an age when so much written English reaches an international readership.

Yet anyone who is using English, whether nationally or internationally, or even just to chat with friends, needs to follow the rules of grammar. Without grammar we could string words together, and in some cases, such as *Me Tarzan, you Jane,* they would be understandable without any grammar. For anything more complex, grammar may be vital. Try to understand this sentence if you can:

Buy car doctor Ford new old the tomorrow will

The words are all English, but the sentence is meaningless because the words have been put in alphabetical order, not grammatical order. It is grammar that turns strings of words into messages with meaning.

Nevertheless when we speak English, specially in informal contexts, we regularly make grammatical "mistakes"; these are a feature of spoken language, with its multiple variants, and most often nobody is bothered by this unless they can't understand what is said. Yet essentially, even when speaking, we *try* to respect the basic grammar of English, because without it what we say would be harder to understand, if not gibberish.

So while grammar is important for almost all forms of language communciation, with **written** language using good grammar may be vital. Written communication is **deferred** or indirect communication, and is *unidirectional*, so there is no opportunity for the receiver to demand verification - at least not under normal circumstances. Proper use of grammar, vocabulary and spelling ensures that messages are immediately comprehensible to the reader, and not meaningless or ambiguous.

The pages of this Descriptive Grammar were initially put together for the benefit of non-native speakers of English, particularly advanced EFL and ESL students, and teachers of English as a foreign or second language. But whether it is learned or taught as a second language or as a first language, English remains the **same** language with the **same** features and difficulties, meaning that this grammar is just as appropriate for native English speakers, be they students or teachers. With linguistic jargon reduced to a minimum, and clear and evidence-based explanations of how English works, this grammar does not confuse readers with terms like *fronted adverbials* or *non-locative PPs*. Such terminology may be relevant for linguistic analysis, but it does little to help teachers to explain grammar - or students to understand it - and may indeed have the opposite effect.

Of course, this grammar is not complete. No grammar is ever complete; it is on the other hand full and covers all the essential points of English grammar likely to be of interest to the lay reader.

Finally, this grammar is the fruit of many years experience. Parts of it were first drafted over twenty years ago, others more recently. All sections have been regularly updated, tested and improved until finally they constitute a full and coherent descriptive overview of English grammar today. Doubtless there will be more changes and improvements in the years to come. Languages never stop evolving.

Andrew Rossiter   *2021*

Table of Contents

1. Verbs

2. The Noun phrase

3. Other parts of speech

4. Sentences and clauses

Note: Use of color in this book.

This grammar makes extensive use of **color coding**. Generally speaking **dark rust red** color is used to highlight the **key words** in any paragraph. When other colors are used, such as scarlet or blue or green, these are essentially to contrast different structures or different categories, or to relate contrastive examples to different cases.

1. Verbs in English

1.1. What are verbs and how are they used?

Verbs are among the essential building blocks of communication in any language. They are one of the two essential elements of a sentence or clause. The other is the subject.

Verbs: a definition

A **verb** exists in relation to a **subject**. It is the key and essential element of the **predicate** in a sentence. The verb expresses an action or process undertaken by or undergone by the subject, or a situation defining the subject.

Actions: to break, to start, to shout

Processes: to sleep, to eat, to think

Situations: to be, to seem,   to live

1.1.1. Verbs in the sentence

Every sentence is made up of a subject and a predicate. The predicate must contain a **verb**, but can contain many other elements too (a complement, an object or more, adverbs, circumstantial expressions, etc.).

Examples

- The president **sneezed.**
- You **have taken the wrong bag.**
- The man and the woman both **forgot.**
- He **forgot to get off the train at Albany.**

1.1.2. Different types of verb

Transitive or intransitive?

Verbs can either be **transitive** or **intransitive**.

- A transitive verb **requires** an object.
- An intransitive verb **cannot have** an object.

Some verbs can be transitive or intransitive, depending on context.

Examples

> Transitive: to send, to employ, to like, to tell
> Intransitive: to sleep, to die, to happen
> **Verbs that can be either**: to give, to burn, to smell

Stative or dynamic?

Verbs can be either **stative** or **dynamic**. Stative verbs describe a situation or state, dynamic verbs describe a process or change of state. The two categories are incompatible with each other.

> **Stative** - describing a state: *to know, to lie, to be, to like,*
>
> **Dynamic** - expressing a change of state: *to discover, to lie down, to become, to learn.*

Examples

> 1) I **know** a lot of people in Chicago.
> 2) My father **likes** beer but not gin.
> 3) The scientists **discovered** a new planet on the edge of the solar system.
> 4) I **sat down** and **went** to sleep.

1.1.3. Tense, aspect, voice

According to conventional modern linguistics, there are only two tenses in English, the present and the past. Other "tenses" are verb *forms* created with the help of auxiliaries and modals. As well as being a rather artificial construct, this can be very confusing for students.

So for the purpose of clarity, it is more useful to use the historic classification of tenses in English, as defined by - among others – the first grammarian of English, Samuel Johnson. Johnson listed **six** English tenses, each of them with a simple and a progressive or continuous aspect.

Here is a table of the main tenses in English, in simple and progressive **aspect**, and active and passive **voices**: sample verb - **to make.**

Aspect voice Tense (form)	Simple active	Progressive active	Simple passive	Progressive passive
Present	I make	I am making	I am made	I am being made
Future with *will*	I will make	I will be making	I will be made	*rare*
Preterit	I made	I was making	I was made	I was being made
Present Perfect	I have made	I have been making	I have been made	*rare*
Past perfect	I had made	I had been making	I had been made	*rare*
Future perfect	I will have made	I will have been making	I will have been made	*rare*

▶ **Present tenses**: for examples, explanations and further details, see §1.2. below: the present tense.

▶ **The future:** for examples, explanations and further details, see § 1.3. below: expressing the future.

▶ **Past tenses**; for examples, explanations and further details on the different past tenses in English, including the "present perfect", see § 1.4. below: past tenses.

Rare forms:

Other "tenses" may exist in English for some verbs, in specific contexts; for example we could envisage *"It will be being repaired "* or "*He's been being looked after*", but forms like this are very rare. Here, nonetheless, is a plausible example of a future progressive passive, which is quite acceptable in this particular case:

> While you're on vacation in Mexico, **I'll be being interviewed** for that job in Philadelphia.

1.1.4. Other verb forms in English: modality

Other forms or tenses, and notably conditionals, are formed with the help of modal verbs: can, could, may, might, would, plus must, should and ought to. These forms are structured in the same way as the future or future perfect. **These are the only structures possible using modal auxiliaries.**

Here is a table of modal verb forms, using the modal auxiliary *must*.

Modality *Aspect*	Modality in the present or future	Modality in the past
Simple, active	I must take	I must have taken
Progressive, active	I must be taking	I must have been taking
Simple, passive	I must be taken	I must have been taken
Progressive, passive	*rare*	*rare*

1.1.5. Moods

Verbs can be used in three different moods

- The indicative (§ 1.2 to § 1.5)
- The subjunctive (§ 1.1.6)
- The imperative (§ 1.7)

Most of the time, verbs are used in the **indicative** mood, which is the normal mood, as illustrated in all the examples above.

As a distinctive verb form, the **subjunctive** is very rare in English, and is normally found only in a few expressions, the most common of which is *If I were you*. See next section - § 1.1.6 below.

The **imperative** is used to give orders, instructions, invitations.

1.1.6. The subjunctive in English

Most English-speakers do not know that there is a subjunctive mood in English; but there is, and many use it quite regularly, without realizing. However there is only one context in which the subjunctive is commonly used, and that is in the context of hypothetical conditional statements. And of these, there is just one recognizably subjunctive expression that is used - from time to time - by most people, and it is:

> If I **were** you *as in* If I were you, I'd drive more carefully.

Note that the expression is "*If I were you*" (a subjunctive), and not "*If I was you*" (an indicative), though the second form is also heard.

With all verbs except *to be,* the **present subjunctive** is **identical** in form to the preterit, to the point that the existence of the present subjunctive as a tense in its own right is largely irrelevant in terms of modern grammar.

1.2. The present tenses in English

1.2.1. Different types of present tense in English

English uses **two** forms of the present, the **Present simple** and **the Present progressive.** This page looks at verbs in the active voice.

► For forms of the present tenses in the passive voice, jump to §1.8. The Passive.

1.2.2. The present simple

In short, the **Present Simple** is used to express:
   a) **permanent** states and permanent truths
   b) **repetitive** actions
   c) **instant** actions (present or future).

Examples – Present simple

> a1) I **like** apples, but I **don't like** oranges.
> a2) I **live** in New York, and I **work** for a big bank.
> a3) Flowers **grow** well in a warm sunny climate.
> a4) Tomorrow never **comes**.
> b1) My brother often **goes** to California.
> b2) It **snows** in winter in New York.
> b3) I **get** up at 6 every morning.
> c1) Oh, I **understand** what you mean.
> c2) And now Messi **gets** the ball, he **shoots**, and he **scores**!
> c3) He **leaves** tomorrow.

1.2.2.1. The present simple affirmative

It is formed using the root form of the verb: there is only one ending to add, an **S** on the third person singular, or **ES** onto verbs ending in **-s**, **-sh, -x,** and **– o.**

Sample verbs	1st sing.	2nd sing.	3rd sing.	1st plural	2nd plural	3rd plural
Bring	I bring	you bring	he, she, it bring**s**	we bring	you bring	they bring
Do	I do	you do	he, she, it do**es**	we do	you do	they do
Pass	I pass	you pass	he, she, it pass**es**	we pass	you pass	they pass

1.2.2.2. The present simple negative

For all verbs, the present simple negative is formed using the root of the verb, and the auxiliary *do* in the negative form: **do not** and **does not** are normally contracted in spoken English, and may also be contracted in the written language.

Sample verbs	1st sing.	2nd sing.	3rd sing.	1st plural	2nd plural	3rd plural
Bring	I do not / don't bring	you do not / don't bring	he, she, it does not / do**es**n't bring	we do not / don't bring	you do not / don't bring	they do not / don't bring
Speak	I don't speak	you don't speak	he, she, it do**es**n't speak	we don't speak	you don't speak	they don't speak

1.2.3. The present progressive

In short, the **Present Progressive** is used to express:
   a) developing situations.
   b) actions that are actually taking place.
   c) **future** actions.

1.2.3.1. The present progressive affirmative

This is formed using the **present participle** of the verb and the present tense of **to be**. The present participle is formed by adding **-ing** to the root (or to the root minus its final *-e* for verbs ending in *e*). The auxiliary is usually contracted in spoken English (as in the second line of the sample verbs table below).

Examples – Present progressive

> a1) John **is getting** better.
> a2) The weather **isn't improving.**
> b1) This week I **am working** in New York.
> b2) Look! That man**'s stealing** my car!
> b3) Slow down, you**'re going** too fast!
> c1) He**'s not going** on vacation **tomorrow**.
> c2) He said he**'s retiring** **next year.**

Sample verbs	1st sing.	2nd sing.	3rd sing.	1st plural	2nd plural	3rd plural
Stand	I am standing	you are standing	he, she, it is standing	we are standing	you are standing	they are standing
Take	I'm taking	you're taking	he, she, it's taking	we're taking	you're taking	they're taking

1.2.3.2. The present progressive negative

The **negative** is formed by adding the particle *not*: there are two different ways of contracting the present progressive negative, as illustrated by the two lines of examples for the verb *take*. Contracted forms are normally used in spoken English, but may sometimes be used in the written language too.

Sample verbs	1st sing.	2nd sing.	3rd sing.	1st plural	2nd plural	3rd plural
Stand	I am not standing	you are not standing	he, she, it is not standing	we are not standing	you are not standing	they are not standing
Take	I'm not taking	you're not taking	he, she, it's not taking	we're not taking	you're not taking	they're not taking
Take		you aren't taking	he, she, it isn't taking	we aren't taking	you aren't taking	they aren't taking

▶ See § 4.5. for more on **negation** in general.

Some verbs are never used in the progressive form

Take care ! some verbs are almost never used in the present progressive - notably certain verbs of permanent state, such as **know, be, like, exist.**

We can say: *I know the plane is arriving late.*
  We cannot say: *I am knowing the plane is arriving late.*

1.2.4. Present simple vs. present progressive:

A contrastive example:

This sentence is a clear example of the difference in usage between the two forms:

> Yes I **eat** hamburgers, but I**'m not eating** a hamburger right now !

1.3. Expressing the future in English

1.3.1. Forms of the future in English

If you talk to a linguist, he or she may tell you that there is no such thing as the "*future tense*" as far as the English language is concerned! There are just two groups of tenses; those that refer to events in past time, and those that talk about the present or the future. But let's not split hairs; for all practical purposes, English, like many other languages, has future tenses: indeed there are **three** ways of using a verb to express the future in English, and one of these is to use the present tense as a future tense.

1.3.2. The present tense used as a future tense

Very often, we use a present tense in English to talk about future events. Look at this short dialogue:

> "Where **are you going** next summer?"
> "We**'re staying** at home. I**'m working** all summer!"
> "Oh what a pity. **Don't** you even get a week off?"
> "Well maybe; we **may go** to Quebec for a couple of days."

Although this dialogue clearly refers to the **future**, the verbs are all in forms of the present. There is no **"will"**, no **"going to".**

Present forms are the simplest way of expressing future time in many cases: the **present progressive** often expresses non-defined time in the future, the **present simple** refers to instant defined moments in time, or events that will occur regularly.

This does not mean that using a clear future tense would be wrong; we could rephrase the previous dialogue using the words **going to** (rather than will) to stress the future nature of events (remembering that going to is actually the present progressive tense of go.)

> "Where **are** you **going to go** this summer?"
> "We**'re going to stay** at home; I**'m going to work** all summer."
> "Oh what a pity. **Aren't** you even **going to get** a week off?"
> "Well maybe **we'll go** to Quebec ...."

But in most contexts, this would sound stilted or **heavy**.

1.3.3. The future with "will" or "going to"

A "future" with will is used to imply **predetermined actions** or **planned or programmed events.** .

> **"Are you coming** home tonight, darling?"
> "Yes; my plane **gets** in at 8.15."
> "O.K. then, I**'ll meet** you at the airport."
> ———
> The President **will** arrive by plane, then he**'ll** go straight to the Capitol.

It is also used to avoid confusion between present and future (e.g. when there is no adverb of time present). Compare**:** *I see* / *I'll see* **or** *I'm there* / *I'll be there.*

Note: the contraction *gonna* (for going to) is only used in spoken English.

1.3.3.1. *Cases* where **will/ going to** must or cannot **be used.**

a) *Will* and *going to* **cannot** be used with the modal verbs **can, could, must, should, would.** If it is essential to mark the future aspect of a modal structure, it is necessary to use **have to** instead of **must**, and **be able to** instead of **can**, as in: *You'll have to do better next time.*

One could also say: *You* **must** *do better next time.*

▶ See also: can, could, must, should

b) They are not used in **time clauses** after **if, when, as soon as, unless, after, before, while** etc, A **"present tense" future** is needed. On the other hand a future with **will** (or *going to*) **IS** required in the **main clause** if the action is in the future. Compare the verbs tenses in these examples.

> **We'll** have a picnic tomorrow **if it's** dry.
> **He'll** open the door **as soon as he hears** the bell.
> **I'll** tell you the rest of the story **when we get** home.

▶ See also: § 1.5. Conditional structures (if clauses).

c) **Take care !** Generally speaking, <u>**will**</u> **is not used in subordinate clauses** when futurity is marked by the verb the main clause. Except in some relative clauses, it is very unusual to find a future tense in both the main clause and a subordinate clause.

> I**'ll sell** it to the first person who **makes** a good offer.
> They**'ll mend** it for you while you **wait**.
> You**'ll do** whatever you**'re told** to do!
> **I'll call you** as soon as I **land** in New York. (**not** will land.)

1.3.4. The future with shall

Shall and the negative form **shan't** are not often used in American English; when they are used, they do more than just express a future action, they express a future **obligation** or **certainty** (or in the negative, a **forbidding**) , and are normally only used in the first person singular (with I), as in:

> I **shall** certainly visit the Guggenhem Museum when I'm in New York.
> I **shan't** be able to come next week, as I'm away on business.

But in both of these examples, **will / won't** are quite acceptable, even preferable, alternatives.

To avoid any risk of error, the simplest principle to adopt is "*never say shall*". Don't use these forms! There is always an alternative.

▶ See also § 1.15: Modal verbs of obligation.

1.3.5. Negative forms of the future

These should not cause any problem for learners of English..
For negative forms of the present tense used with a future meaning, see § 1.2. The present tense.

- The negative forms of **will** are **won't** or **will not.**
- The negative forms of **going to** are **not going to**, with full or contracted forms of the auxiliary.
- (rare) The negative forms of **shall** are **shan't** or **shall not.**

> I **won't** be home for dinner tonight, darling.
> The guard **isn't going to** / is not going to open the doors until 9.
> I **shan't be able to** come next week, as I'm going on vacation.

1.3.6. Other forms and tenses expressing the future

For **passive** forms of future tenses, see §1.8. The passive. For the future perfect tense (as in I will have seen), see below §1.4.5. The future perfect.

1.4. Past tenses in English

The currently popular view of modern linguistics argues that there is only one past tense in English, the "past". This can be very confusing for students, whether they are native speakers or learners of English. It is therefore more coherent to consider the idea of "tense" from the historic and pragmatic viewpoint, that there are **three past tenses** in English - the **simple past** (or preterit), the **present perfect**, and the **past perfect** (or pluperfect).

The three past tenses of English all have simple and progressive forms, as illustrated below. These tenses can be used in the active or the passive.

1.4.1. Forms of past tenses: sample verb make

1. **Simple active** forms

	I	you	he she it one	we	you	they
Simple past	made					
Present perfect	have made	has made		have made		
Past perfect	had made					

2. **Progressive active** forms

	I	you	he she it one	we	you	they
Simple past	was making	were making				
Present perfect	have been making		has been making		have been making	
Past perfect	had been making					

For **passive** forms, ▶ see § 1.8 The Passive.

1.4.2. The simple past (or preterit)

This is used to relate past events in a **historic context.** Often, you will know that it must be used, because the sentence also contains an adverb (or adverb phrase) of time, such as *yesterday*, or a date or time or a time clause like "*when I was younger*".

> 1. Henry Ford **died** *in 1947.*
> 2. The Titanic **sank** *when it hit an iceberg.*
> 3. I **told** you not to drink too much.
> 4. *Next*, they **went** and **cooked** dinner.
> 5. I **liked** that kind of music *when I was a kid.*

1.4.2.1. Simple past - progressive or continuous forms:

Here are some examples with a progressive or continuous form too: both of the events in each sentence are "historic", but one took place while another longer-lasting situation was true:

Examples

> 1. I first **met** my husband when I *was living* in New York.
> 2. The students **shouted** as the President *was speaking*.

1.4.2.2. *Used to* and *would*

The past of finished habit or terminated situation

To express a **finished habit**, or **terminated situation** or action, there are two additional possible structures, one with **used to**, the other with **would**.

To express a **terminated situation**, only the structure with **used to** can be used. Terminated situation can also be expressed using the simple past often reinforced by an adverb of duration or of time.

Examples

> 1. I **used to go** to the Rockies when I was a child, but I don't any longer.
> 2. He **would call** her every day when she was younger, but he doesn't now.
> 3. This street **used to be** very quiet; but now it's full of traffic.
> 4. This street **was once** very quiet, but now it's full of traffic.

1.4.3. The Present Perfect (or compound past)

In British English, the **present perfect** (which Samuel Johnson called quite appropriately, the *compound preterit*) is used to situate past events, or the consequences of past events, **in relation to the present situation** (that's why linguists call it the "present" perfect). **American speakers** do not always use the present perfect in this situation. Sometimes however it must be used (see examples).

Examples

1. I (**have) ordered** a new refrigerator, darling!
   (i.e., the speaker means "*A new refrigerator is coming and will be here soon"*).
2. **I've eaten / I ate** too much!
   (i.e. the speaker implies: "*At this moment now, I do not feel very well; I have a funny feeling in my stomach!*)
3. The Tampa Bay Buccaneers (**have) won** the Superbowl.
   (i.e. *The Tampa Bay Buccaneers are now, at this moment , champions*).

You do not usually find **adverbs of time** used with verbs in the present perfect, but there are some **exceptions**:

    1. already:
    2. adverbs of frequency:
    3. adverbs or adverb phrases of duration related to the present:

Examples

1. Come on, *we ('ve) already started* eating !
2. **I've often seen** people driving too fast down that road.
3. **I've lived** in Seattle **for ten years.**
   (**Contrast with:** *I lived in Seattle for ten years* (but I don't live there now -- a historic statement)
4. **I've lived** in Seattle **since 2005.**
5. **I've been living** in Seattle **since 2005.**   (*Both of these forms are acceptable*)
6. Up to now, **I've always refused** to eat fish.

1.4.3.1. Present-perfect progressive or present-perfect continuous:

These progressive forms are used when we want to imply that an event / events in the past have been continuing until the present point in time, or have taken place over a period of time in the past.

I've been waiting for you since three o'clock.
The doctor **has been seeing** patients for most of the afternoon.

(▶ See § 3.2.2. for more on: *since and for*)

1.4.4. The past perfect or pluperfect.

The past perfect or pluperfect, as in *He had seen*, is normally only used in English when one past event (either a specific action, or a continuous condition) has to be situated *in a more distant pas*t than another past event. In some situations, the progressive or continuous form is necessary.

Examples

> I **had just put** the phone down, when the doorbell rang.
> The man **had been drinking** before the accident happened.
> He **had worked** in the company for five years before he got promotion.

There are some other uses too, but they are less common. Note, for example, the use of the past perfect (and inversion) after **hardly**:

> *Hardly **had I put** the phone down, than the phone rang.*

1.4.5. The future perfect

The future perfect, as in **He will have seen,** is a form that is not common, but is sometimes useful in order to relate two future events or points in time, one of which will be in the past *before* **the other** takes place or is true. It can be used in simple or progressive forms, as in these clear examples.

> I **will have finished** reading the report before **midnight**. *(future perfect simple)*
> He **won't have been climbing** for long before **he reaches** the really difficult part. *(future perfect progressive)*

1.5. The Conditional in English

Conditional clauses in English, after if or unless

1.5.1. Definition of a conditional clause

A conditional clause is a type of subordinate clause, most commonly introduced by the conjunction *if* or *unless*, or occasionally *whether*. Like most subordinate clauses introduced by a conjunction, the conditional clause can either go **before** the main clause, or **after** it.

There are three types of conditional statement in English:

1. **Type 1**: Open conditional   *as in* If you want, you can go home.

2. **Type 2**: Hypothetical conditional *as in* If you wanted, you could go home.
3. **Type 3**: Unfulfilled hypothetical *as in* If you had wanted, you could have gone home.
4. (Hypothetical conditional clauses can also be formed **without if**).

1.5.2. Open *if* clause - the open conditional statement

Open conditional (Type 1) *if* clauses are most commonly used to speak of one event or situation which is conditional on another .

Type 1a. One future event is dependent on another. The verb of the **main** clause is in the **future tense** with "*will*" (or sometimes another modal). The verb of the **conditional** clause is in the **simple present** tense.

Type 1b. One potentially constant state of reality or circumstance is dependent on another. In this case **both verbs** are in the **present** tense.

Type 1c. If the time-frame in the past, both verbs are normally in the simple **preterit**, though sometimes the verb in the conditional clause may be in the past progressive.

1a If you **have** a coffee at night, you **won't sleep** well.
1a If you **finish** in the first ten, you**'ll get** a medal.
1b If I **sleep** well at night, I **feel** much happier next morning.
1b If the temperature **falls** below 32°F, it **freezes**.
1b If it **rains**, everyone **gets** wet.
1c If I **slept** well at night, I **felt** much happier next morning.
1c If it **rained**, everybody **got** wet.
1c Nobody **listened** if he **was shouting** too much

In an open conditional statement, **if** is sometimes replaced by **when**: but there is a difference. Using "**if**" implies that the condition really is open and may not be fulfilled, using "**when**" implies that the condition will / would be fulfilled, that the event will / would really take place.

1.5.3. Open hypothetical conditional statement

We use an open hypothetical conditional (Type 2) **if** clause to refer to a possible future situation which depends on an another possible future situation.

The verb of the **main clause** uses the **present conditional** tense (*would* + infinitive, or *could* +infinitive);

The verb of the **conditional clause** normally uses the **present subjunctive** or **preterit** (these two tenses are identical except with *to be*). Occasionally, the conditional aspect of the statement can be emphasized by using the form *were + to* + infinitive.

1A If you **ate** too much, **you'd (you** would) **get** fatter.
1B You**'d get** fatter if you **ate** too much.
2A If everyone **worked** faster, we **would / could finish** in time.
2B We **wouldn't finish** in time unless everyone **worked** faster.
2C If everyone **were to work** faster, we **would/could finish** in time.
3   If I **went** to London, I **would / could visit** the British Museum.
4.   If you **visited** Wyoming, you **could see** Yellowstone.
5   Unless the directors **increased** sales, **we'd have to** close this
       shop.

Note also this common expression (which uses the open hypothetical form, though it is clearly quite impossible!)

---

6. *If I were you, I'd* .... as in.
    If I **were** you, **I'd go** a bit slower
    If I **were** you, **I'd put** that gun down!!

Open hypothetical structures are also used in cases of **reported or indirect speech**, when reporting an original statement using a type 1 conditional sentence

---

My professor told me **I'd do** much better *if I worked* harder.
   (Original statement: "*You'll* do much better if you **work** harder.")
The magistrate informed him that **he'd go** to prison *unless he stopped stealing.*
   (Original statement: "You'**ll** go to prison unless you **stop** stealing")

The newspaper reported that *unless the directors could increase* sales,
    they'd have to close the shop.

1.5.4. The unfulfilled hypothesis

This refers to a situation in which an event **might have** taken place, but did **not**, because a condition was <u>not</u> fulfilled.

 The verb of the **main** clause goes in the **past conditional** (*would / could etc.* + *have* + past participle).

 The verb of the **conditional** clause is in the **past perfect** (*had* + past participle).

If you **had eaten** too much, you**'d** (you **would) have got** fatter.

You**'d have got** fatter if you**'d eaten** too much.

If everyone **had worked** fast, we**'d have finished** in time (*but we didn't*).

We **wouldn't / couldn't / mightn't** etc. **have finished** in time unless
everyone **had worked** fast (*but we did*).

If I **had gone** to LA, I **could have visited** Universal Studios *(but I didn't)*.

If you **had visited Wyoming**, you **could have seen** Yellowstone *(but you
didn't)*.

Unless we**'d been** very confident of success, we **wouldn't have even
tried.** *(But we were confident, we did try, and we succeeded)*.

Note: using " unless"

"Unless" means the same as "**if ... not**", and has a negative value. It is
frequently (but not only) used in conditional statements where the verb of
the main clause is <u>also</u> in the negative.

You *wouldn't have* **fallen** over **unless** *there'd been* a banana skin on
the ground.

= You **wouldn't have fallen** over **if** there **hadn't been** a banana skin on
the ground.

1.5.5. Omission of "if", with inversion

Sometimes, **hypothetical conditional statements** or **unfulfilled
hypothetical statements** can be expressed <u>omitting</u> the word *if*. When this
happens the **subject** <u>follows</u> the **auxiliary verb** in the <u>conditional</u> clause.

Were the virus to reappear, hospitals would now be ready for it. (open
hypothesis).

= If the virus reappeared, hospitals would now be ready for it. *or* If the
virus were to reappear, hospitals would now be ready for it.

Had I known, I'd never have gone there (unfulfilled hypothesis; implying *"I
did go there because I did not know"*.)
= If I had known, I'd never have gone there.

1.5.6. Whether

Whether is often used in place of *if*, when there is a stated or implied **choice** of conditions. **Whether** is generally required before **or not.**

> I'll stop at midday **whether** I've finished by then **or not**.
>   I wonder **whether / if** it will rain tomorrow **(or not).**

For more about **whether**, see §3.3.3. Correlating coordinators.

1.6. The infinitive in English

The **active present infinitive** - normally known as just "the infinitive" - is the basic or root form of a verb. In English, it can take two forms, with or without the particle *to.* For example:

> **live** or **to live**, **love** or **to love**, **think** or **to think**.

There is also a past infinitive, as in *to have loved.*
▶ See also: § 1.10. Consecutive verbs: gerund or infinitive?

Use of the infinitive

An infinitive cannot be used as the main verb of a sentence: it can only be used in a subordinate infinitive phrase or infinitive clause. Even Shakespeare's most famous expression, "**To be, or not to be?**" is really a subordinate clause. The full sentence is "*To be, or not to be; that is the question.*" or in other words: *"The question is whether to be or not to be".*

1.6.1. The short infinitive, without *to*

This is the **exception**. It is used notably with certain modal auxiliaries, **can, could, may, might, will, shall, could, must.**

> The manager will **need** a vacation.
> When I was younger, I couldn't **read** very well.
> You must **put** on a coat, it's cold outside..

It is also found after a handful of other verbs that introduce a verb complement, in particular: *dare,* verbs of primary perception *see, hear, smell, feel,* and some verbs of permission or causative verbs, notably *make, let* and *have.* Finally there are two common words that are followed by the infinitive without *to*: these are rather and better, in expressions on the model *I'd rather....*

I dare **say** you've never met my brother James.
I heard him **leave** the office by the back door.
I felt her **touch** me very gently on the arm.
I can't make this car **start**.
I'm free!! They let me **go**!
The teacher had the class **redo** the test because he had lost the papers.
You'd better **clean** the kitchen before your mom gets home.
I'd rather **spend** my vacation at the seaside.

After verbs of perception, the second verb can alternatively be a present participle:

I heard him **leave** the house by the front door. *Or*
I heard him **leaving** the house by the front door.

Both these structures are possible, though there may be a shade of difference in meaning between the two; normally the speaker can choose.

1.6.2. The full infinitive, with *to*

The infinitive as verbal complement.

This is the most common use of the infinitive. The infinitive is found in many verbal complements, and notably after the following verbs (among others):

want, wish, have, ought, like, need, hope, expect, fail, pretend, refuse, demand, apply, agree, try.

Examples

I **wish to leave**, and I would **like to go** home.
You **need to see** a doctor as soon as possible.
He **asked to see** the manager, so I **agreed to** let him in.
I fully **expect to finish** the job by this evening.
I **want** you **to tell** me the whole story.
I'm afraid that **I fail to understand** what you are trying to say.

1.6.3. Past infinitives

1.6.3.1. The past infinitive, active.

This is formed using the full present infinitive of the auxiliary *have*, with the past participle of the verb. For example: *to have eaten, to have lost*. Its use is identical to that of the present infinitive. The short form of the past infinitive, without *to*, is only used after modal verbs such as *may, would*. (▶ see § 1 15. Modal verbs).

Examples

> I want **to have finished** the job, before I go home
> You need **to have passed** the test, or else you won't be admitted.
> Uh! You're supposed **to have painted** it blue, not pink!
> I'd like **to have seen** his expression, when he opened the letter!
> I may **have told** you before, I really can't remember.
> Help! I must **have left** my passport in the hotel.

1.6.4. Passive infinitives

These are formed using the full present or past infinitive of the auxiliary *be* with the past participle of the verb. For example: *to be eaten, to have been eaten, to be found, to have been found.* Their use is identical to those of the active infinitives. The short form of the past infinitive, without *to*, is only used after modal verbs such as *may, would*.

Examples

> The car needs **to be cleaned** before you try to sell it.
> The car needs **to have been cleaned** before you try to sell it.
> The mayor likes **to be invited** to official dinners.
> The door appears **to have been left** open all night.
> He seems **to have been given** a very good mark.
> You would **be given** a good mark, if you worked harder.
> I'm sorry, I may **have been recognized**.
> They are very lucky, they could **have been killed**.

1.6.5. Infinitive or gerund?

(▶See also § 1.10: Consecutive verbs: gerund or infinitive.) A few verbs, such as *try, love, prefer, or start* can take a verbal complement either in the form of an infinitive, or as a gerund, with little or no change of meaning. But to avoid a repetition of *-ing*, it is preferable to put the second verb in the infinitive if the first verb is in a progressive form.

1.6.6. Other points

`Take care !`   Two verbs, *remember* and *stop* have different meanings depending on whether the following verb is in the infinitive or is a gerund. As for *forget,* it is normally followed by an infinitive, rarely by a gerund.

> I stopped **to listen** to the music .
> > = *I stopped something else in order to listen to the music.*
>
> I stopped **listening** to the music = *I finished listening to the music.*
>
> I remembered **to do** the shopping
> > = *I did the shopping because I remembered.*
>
> I remember **doing** the shopping = *I know that I did the shopping.*
>
> I forgot **to buy** some milk on my way home.
>
> I forgot (about) **buying** milk on the way home.

1.6.6.1 The infinitive as complement to an adjective.

The infinitive with *to* is found as the complement of certain adjectives, following a comparative adjective, or after adjectives or adverbs qualified by an adverb of degree (*too, enough, so*, etc.).

Examples

> I was pleased **to see** you.
> It was very clever of you **to win** the prize.
> You'd do better* **to choose** a different destination altogether.
> It's easier **to break** it than **to take** it apart.
> The offer really was too good **to be** true.
> It was quite hard **to know** who to believe.
> It was so good of you **to come** quickly.
> We got out of the building quickly enough **to avoid** being seen.

Note: Do not confuse: *You'd better* finish.... with *You'd do better to* finish ....

1.6.6.2. Other uses of the infinitive with to:

The infinitive with *to* is also found as an abbreviation of the form *in order to* + verb:

> I went home **to get** some sleep. *or*
> > I went home **in order to get** some sleep.

Just occasionally, but with a slight change of meaning, it can be found, like a gerund, as the subject of a sentence.

> **To win** the big contract would be a great success.

or to quote a famous line by Oscar Wilde in *the Importance of being Earnest:*

> **To lose** one parent, Mr Worthing, may be regarded as a misfortune; **to lose** both looks like carelessness.

But this is relatively formal style, and also XIXth century English.

1.6.6.3. The infinitive in indirect questions:

The infinitive can also be used to report simple questions in which the interrogative word (i.e. *what* or *where*, etc.) is the direct object of a modal auxiliary *do, can* or *should* referring to future time, and where the original direct question is most often in the first person:

> "**How can I get to Boston**?"
> ► He asked me how he could get to Boston,
>   or: He asked me how to get to Boston.
> "**What do we see next?**"
> ► They asked what they should see next,
>   or: They asked what to see next.

1.6.7. Split infinitives

There is a persistent rumor that it is somehow bad grammar to split infinitives in English. This is absolutely wrong. Infinitives can be split, and have always been able to be split in good English. Indeed, there are cases in which it is virtually **essential** to split infinitives, unless you want to resort to a long and cumbersome paraphrase.

The most famous split infinitive of modern times is the classic introduction to the **Star Trek** TV series, which went:

> These are the voyages of the Starship Enterprise, its 5 year mission to explore strange new worlds, to seek out new life and new civilizations, **to boldly go** where no man has gone before.

In this case the split infinitive is not essential; the text could have said *"to go boldly"*, so in this case there is no compelling reason to use a split infinitive. In other cases, there is. Look at the next example.

> The doctors decided **to rapidly stop** administering pain-killers.

It is not possible to put the word *rapidly* anywhere else in the sentence without either making it **ambiguous**, or else **changing the meaning**. Compare these examples.

> The doctors decided **to rapidly stop** administering pain-killers.
> **Rapidly** the doctors decided to stop administering pain-killers.
> The doctors decided **rapidly** to stop administering pain-killers.
> The doctors decided to stop **rapidly** administering pain-killers.
> The doctors decided to stop administering pain-killers **rapidly**.

The only way in this example to avoid the split infinitive while not changing the meaning is to write a longer periphrase:

The doctors decided they would rapidly stop administering the pain killers.

Great writers and split infinitives

Until the twentieth century, even more so than today, split infinitives were uncommon; but great writers used them from time to time.

> "They had indeed some boats in the river, but they ... served **to just waft** them over, or to fish in them." *Daniel Defoe*
> "Milton was too busy **to much miss** his wife." *Samuel Johnson*

From the 19th century onwards, writers resorted more and more often to using split infinitives; Abraham Lincoln used them, so did Wordsworth, Henry James and Robert Burns – and many more too.

Why do some people object to split infinitives?

The reasons are historical, and invented. The first attempts to describe English grammar reflected principles of Latin grammar, and in Latin as in Greek, splitting an infinitive really is impossible, since the infinitive is a single word (as in *amare* or *legere*). So to make "good" English like Latin, early grammarians decided that the infinitive was something that should not be split. There is no other reason.

In the nineteenth century, traditional grammars continued to claim that splitting infinitives was bad grammar; but writers were using them more and more. Since the early twentieth century, it has become more or less accepted that split infinitives are not just acceptable, but in some cases unavoidable. And why not? An infinitive is a verb form, and in English most verb forms contain two words which can, and in some cases must, be split.

1.7. The imperative in English

1.7.1. Uses of the imperative

The imperative forms of verbs are used for several specific but similar purposes:

- **To give orders or instruct**
- **To warn**
- **To encourage**
- **To invite**

1.7.2. Forms of the imperative

Imperatives are most commonly used in the active and in the **second person**, i.e. implying you. The pronoun is however omitted. They are occasionally used in the first and third persons, with the help of the auxiliary *let*. In all cases, the verb or the auxiliary stands at the start of the sentence.

Sample verb: Look	Affirmative	Negative
Common imperative: second person (you)	*Look*	*Don't look*
First person (I, we)	*Let me look* *Let's wait*	*Don't let me look* *Let's not wait*
Third person (he, she, it, they etc.)	*Let him look (etc.)*	*Don't let him look (etc.)*

Examples: simple imperatives - second person

Tell him to go home.
Shut up!
Give me your answer by Friday!
Don't let any of the prisoners escape.
Don't pretend you never saw anyone enter the house!
Make sure no-one sees you!
Come for dinner tomorrow evening!
Don't hesitate to ask if you need help.

Imperatives and style.

The imperative form by itself can be rather blunt, rather abrupt, even rude. It can be made less abrupt, more polite, by the addition of **softeners** such as *please, would you please*, etc.

Examples: soft imperatives

> **Please tell** him to go home.
> **Would you shut** up!
> **Would you give** me your answer by Friday, please!
> **Please don't let** any of the prisoners escape.
> **Please don't pretend** you never saw anyone enter the house!

First and third person imperatives are not common, but there are some common expressions that use them.

> **Let** me **see**!
> **Let's go.**
> **Let's** not **wait** any longer.
> **Let** him **think** what he wants!

Passive imperatives

These are rare: here are a couple of examples:

> **Don't be taken** by surprise!   **Let** them **not be** forgotten.

1.7.3. Emphatic imperatives

There are two ways of adding emphasis to an imperative.

- Occasionally the pronoun **you** is added to simple imperatives, in order to add emphasis or to specify to whom the imperative is addressed. See examples 1 - 4
- Alternatively **do** can be added at the start of the sentence, as a redundant auxiliary. See examples 5 - 7

Examples

1. *You* wait until your turn!
2. Shut up, *you*!
3. *You* wait here while I go for help!
4. *You* watch the front door, and you watch the back!
5. *Do* pour another coffee, if you'd like to.
6. *Do* put that gun down please, you're frightening people!
7. Oh *do* shut up!

The examples with added **you** may not look like emphatic imperatives, but they are. The **you**s can be omitted, and the meaning remains the same. They are thus optional, not required as in an indicative context.

1.8. Voices – active and passive

1.8.1. Usage

In European languages, including English, verbs can be used in two different "voices", called the **active** and the **passive.** The active voice is by far the more common of the two. Here are some simple examples of verbs used in the active voice.

Box A: Examples – sentences expressed in the active voice.

> 1.   I **love** football.
> 2.   The people **were talking** very loudly.
> 3.   President Roosevelt **wrote** reports every day.
> 4.   James **hit** the ball very hard.

Most sentences can be expressed without any need to use forms of the passive; however sometimes we may want to change the way a sentence is expressed, in order to imply a slightly different meaning. Generally speaking, it is only **transitive** sentences (sentences that have a direct object) that can be rephrased in the passive.

So let's look at the same four examples again, reexpressed using a passive verb, *when this is possible.*

Box B: the same sentences expressed in the passive.

> 1.   Football **is loved** by me..... *No!* *this sounds very strange! It would never be said, even if it is technically possible.*
> 2.   This sentence cannot be rephrased in the passive.. **Talk** *is an intransitive verb.*
> 3.   Reports **were written** every day by President Roosevelt `OK.`
> 4.   The ball **was hit** very hard by James. `OK.`

The **passive** is used, essentially, in three situations:

- To put more **emphasis** on the word that would be the object of an active sentence.
- To write an **impersonal** sentence.
- To simplify the **structure** of a complex sentence.

Let's see examples of these three situations.

1.8.2. Using the passive for emphasis

Now let's compare sentences 3 and 4 from boxes A and B above.

<table>
<tr><td>3a.</td><td>President Roosevelt wrote reports every day.</td></tr>
<tr><td>3b.</td><td>Reports were written every day by President Roosevelt.</td></tr>
<tr><td>4a.</td><td>James hit the ball very hard.</td></tr>
<tr><td>4b.</td><td>The ball was hit very hard by James.</td></tr>
</table>

Sentences 3a and 4a describe human actions – which is what most everyday sentences do.

Sentences 3b and 4b describe the same actions, but place **objects** (*reports / ball*) at the center of the action, by making them into the subject of passive sentences.

In these normal "passive transformations" the **direct object** of the active sentence becomes the **subject** of the passive sentence.

Occasionally however, instead of the direct object, it is the **indirect** object of an active sentence that can become the subject of a passive sentence. For details on this see ▶ § 1.8.6. the Passive followed by an object, below.

1.8.3. Using the passive to make an impersonal sentence

In this case, the passive is used as a tool of formal **style** (see § 4.9. styles) to express actions that are not specifically linked to any person. We can thus remove the person from sentences 3b and 4b, which then become non-personal, and rather **formal**.

<table>
<tr><td>3c. Reports were written every day.</td></tr>
<tr><td>4c. The ball was hit very hard.</td></tr>
</table>

Here are two other examples of formal non-personal use of the passive.

<table>
<tr><td>5.</td><td>The students were told to assemble at 9.30 a.m.</td></tr>
<tr><td>6.</td><td>A public meeting will be held in the Town Hall next Friday.</td></tr>
</table>

In these examples, the writer does not tell us – maybe does not want to tell us – who has told the students to assemble, nor who is organising a public meeting. Either it is not important, or the writer prefers not to say.

1.8.4. Using the passive to simplify sentence structure

Often, meaning is easier to understand if we use the **same** subject for a sequence of sentences or clauses: sometimes, this may require the use of a passive structure for one or more of the clauses.

Examples - using a passive to simplify a sequence of clauses.

> 1a. I arrived in Denver. My brother **met** me at the airport.
> 1b. I arrived in Denver **and was met by** my brother at the airport.
> 2a. The guests were waiting for an hour before someone **gave** them a drink.
> 2b. The guests were waiting for an hour **before they were given** a drink.

1.8.5. Forms of the passive

Most of the active forms of transitive verbs, including the infinitive and the imperative, have equivalent forms in the passive. But **intransitive verbs** cannot be used in the passive.

Here is a table of examples for the verb **to help**.

Form / Tense *Aspect, voice*	Simple, active	Progressive, active	Simple, passive	Progressive, passive
Present	I help	I am helping	I am helped	I am being helped
Future	I will help	I will be helping	I will be helped	*rare*
Preterit	I helped	I was helping	I was helped	I was being helped
Present Perfect	I have helped	I have been helping	I have been helped	*rare*
Past perfect	I had helped	I had been helping	I had been helped	*rare*
Future perfect	I will have helped	I will have been helping	I will have been helped	*rare*

For more details see pages on the Present (§ 1.2.), the Past (§ 1.4.), and the Future(§ 1.3.). The passive can also sometimes be formed using the verb get, instead of **be**, as an auxiliary. (► See § 1.14 Get and got).

1.8.6. The passive followed by an object

Unlike in some other European languages, passive verb forms in English can sometimes be followed by a direct object. This is only possible when the indirect object of an active sentence becomes the subject of the passive sentence.

This happens with a **limited number of verbs**, known as "ditransitive verbs" among the most common of which are *give, tell, bring, teach, ask, pay, sell, send*,

Active sentences	Passive equivalent
The doctor gave **me** some medicine	I was given **some medicine** by the doctor.
Laura told **the children a story**.	**The children** were told **a story** by Laura.
They brought **the lady a Christmas card**	**The lady** was brought **a Christmas card.**
Mr. Diaz taught **me English**	I was taught **English** by Mr. Diaz.
The tourists asked **me a question**.	I was asked **a question** by the tourists.
My sister made **me a chocolate cake**.	I was made **a chocolate cake** by my sister.
The company paid **$200 to each man**.	**Each man** was paid **$200** by the company.
The mayor sent **a letter to the residents.**	**The residents** were sent **a letter** by the mayor.

1.9. Gerunds and -ing words

Gerunds, verbal nouns or present participles ending in -ing

▶ See also § 1.10: Consecutive verbs.

1.9.1. The different types of word ending in -ing:

The English language does not use many grammatical "endings", but some of those it does use have several different functions. The *-ing* ending is one of them. Words ending in *-ing* can be gerunds, verbal nouns, or present participles. **Distinguishing** (= *gerund*) between these, and using them correctly is not always easy – until you understand these three simple rules.

Definitions

The gerund is a verb which is used as if it were a noun (Examples 1 & 2 below). Since it is a verb, it can **not** be qualified by an adjective, nor preceded by an article, but, like other forms of the verb, it can be modified by an adverb and take a complement.

A **verbal noun** (Examples 3 & 4) is a **noun** formed from a verb; some verbal nouns end in -**ing**.
Verbal nouns, like other nouns, <u>can</u> take a determiner, and be qualified by adjectives.

A **participle** is an adjective or part of a participial phrase qualifying a noun or a pronoun. (Examples 5 et 6). The present participle is also used in the **progressive** aspect of verb tenses (Examples 7 & 8).

See the differences of use that are illustrated by these examples.

Words in -ing: Gerund, noun or present participle (and progressive verb form)

---

1. **Seeing** is **believing**.
2. **Living** cheaply in New York is quite possible.
3. The book was easy **reading**!
4. He managed to make a good **living**.
5. **Smiling**, the lady told them they'd won the big prize.
6. I heard them **arguing** last night.
7. I'm **taking** my brother to the station tonight
8. The man was **phoning** his friend, when the lights went out.

1.9.2. The gerund in English: a verb used as a noun

The **gerund** in English has the form of the present participle in *-ing*.
It is the most common form of the verb used as a noun, and can be the subject (examples 1 to 7 below), or the object of a sentence (8 & 9, 14 to 16) , or follow prepositions (10 to 13).

Examples of gerunds

1. **Seeing** is believing.
2. **Reading** that book was very interesting.
3. **Drinking** is essential.
4. **Drinking** too much pop can make you fat.
5. **Taking** the bus was rather a good idea.
6. **Swimming** is very good exercise.
7. **Taking** too many aspirins is dangerous.
8. I really like **sailing**.
9. This article needs fully **rewriting**.
10. He drove two hundred miles without ever **stopping**.
11. I look forward to **seeing** you again next week.
12. I'm thinking of **painting** my house.
13. I started by carefully **turning** off the electricity.
14. Do you mind **shutting** the window, please?
15. Will you consider **taking** the job?
16. I've really enjoyed **meeting** you.

As the examples above show, the gerund is a verb used <u>as if it were</u> a noun, but **not in the same way as** a noun. In other words, **it keeps its verbal qualities.** Since it **is not a noun**, it cannot be qualified by an adjective; on the contrary, it keeps some of the essential features that distinguish a verb, notably that it can take a direct object (examples 2, 4, 7, 11 - 16 above) , and/or be qualified by an adverb (examples 6, 9 & 13).

When gerunds are used as **verbal complements** (second verbs following a first verb), as in examples 8 and 9 above, they can often be rephrased using an infinitive instead of the gerund (For example: *"This article needs to be fully rewritten".*. using a passive infinitive).

However a few verbs require a gerund, not an infinitive (Examples 14 - 16 above). The most common of these are *admit, consider, dislike, deny, enjoy, finish, involve, miss, mind, suggest,*

▶ For more details on this, see Appendix - Consecutive verb structures at the end of this book.

1.9.3. Verbal nouns: nouns that are derived from verbs

There are a large number of ways of creating a noun from a verb: among the most common of these are words that use the root form of the verb and a noun ending such as -**ment** (as in *achievement*), -**ance** (as in *disappearance*), -**ion** (as in *confirmation*) , or -**ing** (as in *The changing of the guard.*) You can see that these -ing forms really are **nouns**, not verbs, as they can be qualified by adjectives

***Examples of** verbal nouns:*

1. That is a very nice **painting**.
2. We're going to see the **changing** of the guard at Buckingham Palace.
3. After a slow **beginning**, the show got a bit more lively.
4. This story has a rather unexpected **ending**.
5. The commission demanded the **breaking** up of the corporation into two separate units.
6. The last **meeting** was not very productive.

1.9.4. Areas of possible confusion

Sometimes it is difficult to decide if a word is a gerund or a verbal noun; and in fact, the quality of the -**ing** word can change *according to context*. Look at these examples:

Examples

1. For musicians, **practicing** is essential.
2. For musicians, **practicing** an instrument is essential
3. For musicians, regular **practicing** is essential.
4. NO ~~For musicians, **regular practicing an instrument** is essential~~.
5. For musicians, **regularly practicing** an instrument is essential.
6. For musicians, the regular **practicing** of an instrument is essential.

In examples **1** and **2** above, *practicing* is clearly a **gerund**; in example 2 it is followed by a complement, *an instrument*.

But in example **3** it is preceded by an adjective *regular*, so this time it is being used differently, as a **verbal noun**.

We can verify this if we try to add a complement, as in example **4**. **It is not possible.** We cannot say "~~For musicians, regular practicing an instrument is essential~~.". **An *-ing* word cannot simultaneously be preceded by an** adjective and followed by a direct complement. Other solutions are needed; the *ing* word must **either** be used as a gerund, **or** as a verbal noun, but **not both at once**.

So while example **4** does not work, there are two solutions.

Example **5** uses the word *practicing* as a gerund, as in examples 1 and 2; and being a gerund, it is modified by an adverb, *regularly*.

Finally, example **6** rephrases example 5, but using *practicing* as a verbal noun, not a gerund. We can see that it is a noun, as it is now part of a noun phrase introduced by an article and including an adjective.

1.9.5. Present participles

Participles are adjectives; they can either stand alone, before or after their noun, as the situation requires, or else they can be part of an adjectival phrase.

Participles are often used to make a shortened form of a subordinate clause, as in examples 1 and 3 below,

In example 1 below, *Looking out of...* is an ellipsis or contraction of **As I was** *looking out of...*, and *... I saw the tornado coming* is a contraction of *...I saw the tornado **that was** coming*.

Elliptical phrases may come before the noun or pronoun (e.g. *Looking out of the window, I saw ....*) or after it (e.g. *I saw the tornado coming*).

However, when the participle phrase is a shortened form of a relative clause, it **MUST** come after the noun (examples 4 & 7 below).

Present participles are also used to form the progressive forms of present and past tenses as in Examples 8 – 10 below:

Examples of present participles:

1. **Looking** out of the window, I saw the tornado **coming**.
2. In the course of the **coming** week, I have three interviews to go to.
3. I saw the child **standing** in the middle of the road.
4. The people **living** next door are very friendly.
   NO 4b ~~The living next door people are very friendly~~ is impossible.
5. This is a seriously **interesting** book.
6. The **winning** team will go through to the finals.
7. The team **winning** in the first round will go through to the finals.
8. I was **looking** out of the window when I saw the tornado
9. At the moment, he's **living** in Boston.
10. The company has been **doing** very well for the past two years.

1.9.6. -ing forms in passive structures

Gerunds and participles are most commonly used in the active voice; they can however be easily used in the passive too.

Examples 1 - 3: are **gerunds**, **examples 4 & 5** are **participles**.

Examples

1. **Being seen** is more important than **being heard**.
2. He drove two hundred miles without ever **being stopped**.
3. They began their trip by **getting** hopelessly **lost**.
4. Everyone watched the building **getting demolished**.
5. At the moment they're **being sold** at half price.

1.10. Consecutive verbs in English

When to use an -ing form, and when to use an infinitive

> **Definitions**
> **Consecutive** verbs, also called **catenative verbs** or **linked verbs**, are verbs that can be followed **directly** by a second verb, the second verb being normally the **object** of the first.
>   Depending on the first verb used, the second verb will be in the form of a gerund (see § 1.9.2.) or of an infinitive with *to* (see § 1.6.2.). With a few verbs, there is a choice of structures; with most there is no choice.

While the definition of consecutive verbs applies also to auxiliaries and modal verbs, these are used differently, so are best considered as separate categories. These are treated on their own pages: See ▶ be, have, get and modal auxiliaries of obligation or possibility.

1.10.1. Gerund or infinitive? The main principles

Many learners of English have difficulty knowing whether the second verb in a linked verb pair should be a gerund in *-ing*, or an infinitive with **to**. As these common examples show, different verbs use different structures. For a full list of main consecutive verbs, see Appendix at the end of this book.

Examples

> I **want to learn** English fast! *(with want a full infinitive is needed)*
> I **keep getting** confused by this question! *(with keep a gerund is needed)* .
> I **love meeting** my friends in the coffee shop after work!
> I **love to meet** my friends in the coffee shop after work! *(with love either a gerund or a full infinitive can be used).*

Confused? That's understandable! But luckily there are a couple of general principles that will help you know which structure to use.

- **Type 1** verbs: When the first verb is **prospective**, i.e. it looks (or looked) towards the future, the second verb is the consequence or follow-on of the first verb. In this case the second verb can almost always – and with many verbs must – be used in the form of an **infinitive with to**:

- **sample verbs**: *ask, decide, expect, hope, intend, need, plan, promise, want,*

The secretary **asked to go** home early
I **decided to take** the train instead of the car.
I e**xpect to be** home late tonight.
I **intend to buy** a new car some time this year.
We **need to go** to the supermarket before it shuts.
They **plan to open** three new shops in Kentucky this year.
I **promise not to tell** anyone !
I **want to learn** English fast !

- **Type 2 verbs.** When the first verb **expresses an emotion, a permanence, or a principle,** the second verb is most likely to be in the form of **a gerund**. Sample verbs: be afraid / tired of ... etc. , can't stand, detest, dislike, enjoy, hate, keep, keep on, like, love.

The secretary was tired **of working** late every evening.
I can't stand **listening** to that man hour after hour !
He detests / hates / loves **getting** up early in the morning.
I very much dislike **having to** tell you everything three times !
The children really enjoy **going** to see their grandparents.
Doctor, I keep **getting** this terrible pain in my arm !
He kept on **reading** until he went to sleep.

Other verbs. Not all consecutive verbs are type 1 or type 2. Several other consecutive or catenative verbs do not fit into either of these types. There are also verbs of **obligation** or **prevention**, and **causative** verbs, which are not really consecutive verbs, as the two verbs are **always separated** in <u>active</u> structures by a noun or pronoun. See ▶ § 1.17.1. Verbs of authority.

Infinitive without to? **No**! Let's not make things complicated! Unlike modals (*will, can* etc.), and with one exception, no consecutive verbs need to be followed by a short infinitive without to! The exception is **let**, which **is always** followed by a short infinitive. But apart from a few idiomatic phrases such as *Don't let go*, or the title of the James Bond novel *Live and let die*, let is not a consecutive verb, and cannot be directly followed by a second verb. Just a few other verbs **can be** used consecutively and followed by a short infinitive without to (**dare, help, go** ...) but this is optional, an exception to the rule, not another structure.

> I **was told to go** home.
> My brother **was taught to speak** English by Mrs. Jones.
> **He was believed to be** in New York at the time.
> The **child was seen getting** into a black car.
> **We were asked** to be ready by six thirt y

However **in active statements**, **the direct object** of the first verb, which must be at least a **noun or pronoun,** must come **before** the second verb of which it is also the **subject**.

> The boss **told me to go** home.
> Mrs. Jones **taught my brother to speak** English.
> People **believed him to be** in New York at the time.
> Someone **saw the child getting** into a black car.
> **They asked us to be** ready by six thirty.

Verbs that are used like this are not consecutive verbs, but normal (non-consecutive) verbs followed by an infinitive phrase or a gerund phrase.

1.11. The verb to be

Forms

Person		Present	Preterit	Present perfect	Past perfect	Future
1st sing	I	am	was	have been		will be (shall be)
2nd sing	you	are	were	have been		will be
3rd sing	he, she, etc.	is	was	has been	had been	
1st plural.	we	are	were	have been		will be (shall be)
2nd plural	you	are	were	have been		will be
3rd plural	they	are	were	have been		

1.11.1. Functions: to be as a main verb

The verb *to be* is the fundamental verb used to indicate the existence of an entity (person, object, abstraction) or to relate an entity to its qualities or characteristics. In linguistics, it is sometimes known as a *copula*.

Unlike transitive verbs, it does not take a direct object, but a complement, since the subject and complement of the verb *to be* relate to the same entity. The complement of *to be* can be a noun, a noun group, an adjective, or a prepositional phrase.

Examples of usage of the verb to be as main verb

> That man **is** the boss.
> That man **is** the winner of last year's Nobel Prize for physics.
> That man **is** very intelligent
> That man **is** in rather a difficult situation
> I **have been** here before
> She **was** much prettier in her younger days.
> The three people **were** all brothers.
> The man **had been** in the water for an hour, before anyone found him.
> I'**ll be** home by six at the latest, darling !
> There'**ll be** at least 200 people at the concert tonight.

1.11.2. Functions: to be as an auxiliary

Progressive or continuous aspect formed with to be

The verb **to be** is used as an auxiliary to denote the **progressive** or **continuous** aspect of an action; it is thus used to form the "present progressive" (§ 1.2.3.) and "past progressive" and other progressive tenses (also called the present continuous and past continuous tenses, etc.). In this case, **be** is followed by the **present participle** of a verb.

> We*'re waiting* for the match to begin.
> We *have been waiting* for you for two hours.
> They *won't be giving* him a prize for his work this time.

Model "stand"	Present progressive	Future progressive	Preterit progressive	Present perfect progressive	Past perfect progressive
1st sing	I am stand-ing	I will be standing	I was stand-ing	I have been standing	I had been standing
2nd sing	you are standing	You will be standing	You were standing	You have been standing	You had been standing
3rd sing	he / she... is standing	He / she ... will be standing	He/ she ... was stand-ing	He / she... have been standing	he / she ... had been standing
1st plural	we are standing	We will be standing	We were standing	We have been standing	We had been standing
2nd plural	you are standing	You will be standing	You were standing	You have been standing	You had been standing
3rd plural	they are standing	They will be standing	They were standing	They have been standing	They had been standing

Other tenses can be formed, including tenses with modal auxiliaries:

examples *I could have been standing - They must have been standing.*

1.11.3. Passive forms with be

The verb **to be** is also used as an auxiliary to form **passive tenses**. In this case, the auxiliary **be** is followed by the **past participle** of a verb.

Sample verb "Take"	Present simple passive	Future passive	Preterit passive	Present perfect passive	Past perfect passive
1st sing	I am taken	I will be taken	I was taken	I have been taken	I had been taken
3rd sing	It... is taken	He / she ... will be taken	He / she ... was taken	He / she ... has been taken	He / she ... had been taken
Etc					

Other tenses can be formed, including tenses with modal auxiliaries.

**Examples

> You could have been seriously injured.
> They must have been told the truth.

1.11.4. Progressive tenses in the passive

As **to be** is used both to form passive tenses, and tenses with progressive aspect, it follows that it is used *twice* in verb forms that are both passive <u>and</u> progressive.

While a complete range of tenses is theoretically possible, in practice English only has **two passive progressive tenses**, the present progressive passive, and the past progressive passive.

Sample verb "**help**"	Present progressive passive	Past progressive passive
1st sing	I am being helped	I was being helped
3rd sing	It... is being helped	He / she ... was being helped
Etc.		

1.11.5. Get used instead of be in passive forms

In everyday English, the auxiliary *be* is often replaced by *get* to express a verb in the passive, whether in progressive or simple aspect.

> She *was being / was getting* taken to hospital, when suddenly she felt
>   much worse.
> The computer network is down, as the server *is being/ is getting*
>   changed.
> The window *is being / is getting* mended.
> The staff *were being* given their daily instructions.
> Next I *was taken / got taken* to see the director of human resources.

1.11.6. Avoid confusion

Remember that when the auxiliary **to be** is followed by a **present** participle, the verb is in the **active voice**; when it is followed by a **past** participle, the verb in in the **passive voice.**

The chicken **was eating** its dinner.
  The chicken **was eaten** for dinner.
They **were telling** the truth, when they said that they knew nothing.
  They **were told** the truth, when the man finally confessed.
The women **have been asking** to see the general manager.
  The women **have been asked** to see the general manager.

1.11.7. The verb to be as a modal verb

The verb to be is occasionally used as a modal auxiliary; but in this it is a strange verb, as it can have either a value of futurity, or a value of obligation, or something between the two, supposition.

In the first and third persons, it is a modal whose most common value is futurity: in the second person, its main value is one of obligation. However, this distinction is not always true.

Person		Present	Preterit
1st sing.	I	I am to make	was to make
2nd sing	you	You are to make	were to make
3rd sing	he, she, etc.	... is to make	was to make
1st plural.	we	... are to make	were to make
2nd plural	you	... are to make	were to make
3rd plural	they	... are to make	were to make

In other words, while "*I'm to get a new car next week*" would normally mean "*I'm **going to** get a new car next week*" (futurity), "**You're** *to go to Detroit next week*" would normally mean "*You **should** go to Detroit next week*" (mild obligation). However, in many cases, ambiguity is possible, even if **context usually clarifies the meaning.**

1. The plane **was to** leave at 8 (meaning: The plane *was supposed* to leave at 8).

2. I**'m to** work in Los Angeles next year (I'm *going to / have to* work in Los Angeles.....).

3. I**'m to** make three of these cakes (I *must / am supposed to* make three.....).

4. He**'s to** stand as candidate for the presidency (He *is going to* stand.....).

5. The children **were to** stay at home that afternoon (The children *were meant* to or *were going to* .....).

6. After that, they **were to** get lost. (After that, they *were going to* get lost).

7. After that, they **were to** go home (After that, *they were supposed to* go home).

8. You**'re to** get better marks next time. (You ***must*** get better marks ....).

9. When you get home, you**'re to** go straight to bed. (When you get home, you *must* go straight to bed).

1.12. The verb to have

Forms functions and usage

The verb **have** is one of the two most frequently used verbs in English. It can be used in three different functions in the sentence.
   1. As a main verb
   2. As an auxiliary verb, and
   3. As a modal auxiliary verb.

1.12.1. Have as a main verb

The verb *to have* is one of the core verbs of the English language, and can be used to express possession ownership or acquisition.

In this usage, it is a transitive verb, and must therefore be followed by a direct object. The direct object of *to have* can be a noun, a noun group, a pronoun or a numeral, or sometimes by a secondary clause.

1.12.1.1. Affirmative forms of the main verb to have

Person	1st / 2nd sing	3rd sing	Plural
Tense	I / you	he, she, etc.	we / you / they
Present.	have	has	have
Future	will have		
Preterit	had		
.Present perfect	have had	has had	have had
Past perfect	had had		

1.12.1.2. Abbreviated forms of *have*:

As a main verb, **have** and **has** are **not** normally abbreviated , though shortened forms **'ve** or **'s** are found in some common expressions such as *"I've an idea".*

Abbreviated forms are more common with the present perfect and past perfect forms, but note that in this case it is the auxiliary that is shortened, not the main verb which always remains **had**. (Example: *We'd all had a good time*). More examples below.

1.12.1.3. Negative forms of the main verb to have.

Take care: The normal negative forms of the main verb **have / has** are **do not have** and **does not have**, or their shortened forms. These are <u>not</u> the same as the normal negative forms of the <u>auxiliary</u> or <u>modal</u> verb **have**. The forms *haven't, hasn't, (have not, has not)* etc. are **not** normally used as negative forms of the <u>main verb</u> **have**.

Contracted forms can be used in all styles of English, oral and written, except for the most formal.

Person	1st / 2nd sing	3rd sing	Plural
tense	I / you	he, she, etc.	we / you / they
Present.	do not have / don't have	does not have/ doesn't have	don't have
Preterit	did not have / didn't have		
.Present perfect	haven't had	hasn't had	haven't had
Past perfect	hadn't had		

Exceptions: There are some exceptions where the negative form of the main verb *have* uses the negative structure of the auxiliary, notably some common expressions such as *I haven't a clue* (= I don't know) or *I haven't the time*; but even with this second possible exception, it would be more normal to say *I don't have (the) time* or *I haven't got time.*

Examples of use of the verb have as main verb

1. I **have** an idea. *(possession)*
2. My father **has** three brothers and two sisters.
3. The doctor **had** a lot of experience.
4. He **has** three Cadillacs and a Tesla. *(ownership)*
5. Where are the scissors? Do you **have** them?
6. The house **has** eight windows and three doors.
7. **I've had** three phone calls so far today. *(acquisition)*
8. Before getting into his car, he**'d had** six glasses of whisky....
9. "Romeo and Juliet" doesn't **have** a happy ending.
10. I**'ll have** chicken and ginger with fried rice please.
11. Make sure that the children **have** what they need.
12. I **don't have** any brothers or sisters.
13. We **haven't had** any complaints so far.

1.12.2. Have or have got?

Particularly in **spoken** English, **have** as a main verb, meaning *own* or *possess or receive* can be consolidated by **adding** the participle **got**. Here are the same example sentences, consolidated by got when this is a possible alternative – notably in the present tense.

Replacing the past form had by **got** is a different question. Though it is sometimes possible when had means *received* (=acquisition), in other cases *(in italics)* this change of verb is either **impossible**, or will change the meaning of what is being said, or make it ambiguous. My father **has got** three brothers and two sisters.

1. *I***'ve got** *an idea.*
2. My father**'s got** three brothers and two sisters

3. *The doctor **had** a lot of experience.* (had = possessed)
   The doctor ***had gotten*** a lot of experience. (*had gotten= had acquired*)

4. He**'s got** three Cadillacs and a Tesla.

5. Where are the scissors? **Have** you **got** them?

6. The house **has got** eight windows and three doors.

7. **I got** three phone calls today.

8. Before getting into his car, he**'d had** six glasses of whisky.... (*had = drunk*)

9. "Romeo and Juliet" is a tragedy; it **hasn't got** a happy ending.

10. I**'ll have** chicken curry with fried rice please.

11. I **haven't got** any brothers or sisters.

12. We **haven't got** any complaints so far.

13. If he **hadn't had** those mushrooms, he wouldn't be ill. (*had = eaten*)

▶ For more about this, see § 1.14 Get and got

1.12.3. Have as an auxiliary

1.12.3.1. Past verb forms using have

The verb **have** is used as an auxiliary to form the present perfect and past perfect forms of other verbs.

Sample verb "walk"	1st sing	2nd sing	3rd sing	Plural
Present perfect	I have walked	you have walked	he / she... has walked	we / you / they have walked
Past perfect	I had walked	You had walked	He/ she ... had walked	we / you / they had walked
Present perfect progressive	I have been walking	You have been walking	He / she... have been walking	we / you / they have been walking
Past perfect progressive	I had been walking	You had been walking	he / she ... had been walking	We had been walking

Other tenses can be formed, including the **future perfect** (simple and progressive – see §1.4.5.) and tenses with modal auxiliaries. These are not common though they may be useful in some cases.

I **will have walked** ten miles today by the time I get home. (future perfect
    simple)
I **will have been walking** for three hours by the time I get home. (future
    perfect progressive)
I **could have been walking** on the beach instead of sitting in the car.
    They **must have walked** all the way home.

1.12.3.2. Contracted forms of the auxiliary verb *have*

As an auxiliary, **have**, **has** and **had** are frequently contracted to the forms
've, 's and **'d**, when this is possible - i.e. after pronouns - , but it depends on
the type of English used.

- **In written English**, contracted forms are possible but **unusual** after
  pronoun subjects;   contracted forms are **not used** after noun subjects.
- **In oral / spoken English** contracted forms are **normal** but not
  essential.
- After pronoun subjects, even in formal speech, even the Queen of
  England would be likely to say "*I've had a good day*", rather than "*I
  have had a good day.*"
- However after noun subjects, contracted forms may be heard, even
  if they would not be written: for example,
  A newspaper journalist would write
    "*The President has appointed a new team.*"
  but a TV journalist would say:
    "*The President's appointed a new team.*"

1.12.3.3. Negative forms of the auxiliary verb *have.*

The standard negative forms of the **auxiliaries** **have, has** and **had** are
haven't, hasn't and **hadn't.**

  Example: *I haven't finished my lunch*. More examples below.

Take care: Forms using do (*don't have, doesn't have* etc.) are **never** used
as negative forms of the **auxiliary** verb have, only of the **main** verb have.
(see above).

Ain't

Also note the word **ain't**, a colloquial alternative to both **isn't** and **aren't** as well as **hasn't** or **haven't**, as used in the Rolling Stones' classic hit *"I ain't got no satisfaction"*.

1.12.3.4. Passive forms

Verb forms using the auxiliary **have** can also be put into the passive.

Sample verb "take"	Present perfect passive	Past perfect passive
1st sing	I have been taken	I had been taken
3rd sing	He / she ... has been taken	He / she ... had been taken

Other tenses can be formed, including tenses with modal auxiliaries.

Examples:

> You **could have been** seriously injured.
> They **must have been** dreaming.

Different examples of use of the verb *have* as an auxiliary

1.   I **have** finished my lunch / I**'ve** finished my lunch.
2.   The president **has** chosen his new team.
3.   The president**'s** chosen his new team *(this form is possible in spoken language, but it would not normally be written)*.
4.   The children **had** gone home five minutes earlier than usual.
5.   The captain **had** told his team to play hard in the final minutes of the game.
6.   The president **has not** yet arrived / The president hasn't yet arrived
7.   Until I lived in San Francisco, I **hadn't** been on a streetcar.
8.   **Have** you seen the light Mr. Jones?
9.   **Hasn't** the rain stopped yet?

1.12.3.5. The verb *have to* as a modal verb

For information on "have to" as a modal verb, see § ► 1.15.1. Modals of obligation below.

1.13. The verbs to do and to make

Make and **Do** are among the commonest verbs in the English language. Native English speakers do not mix them up; but they can cause difficulty for speakers of other languages, as many other languages have a single verb that corresponds to *both* do *and* make in English.

Spanish **hacer**, French **faire**, German **machen**, Italian **fare**, Russian **делать**, Portuguese **fazer**.... they can all mean either *do* or *make* in English. And to complicate things even more for non-native speakers, the English language also has the expression *to make do with* !

1.13.1. Meanings and use of do and make

The fundamental difference between **do** and **make** is that:

Expressions with **do** generally focus on a **process;**

Expressions with **make** focus on the **result** of a process.

- **Do** is generally used in expressions that express **actions**:
  Examples: *do the shopping, do your best, do a competition, do something very stupid…*
  In the expression "**do the shopping**", the focus is on the action, i.e. buying things in shops.

- **Make** is generally used in expressions which focus on the **result**, something that is created, acquired or expressed.
  Examples: *make a shopping-list, make a mistake, make lunch, make a lot of noise, make money*
   In the expression *"make a shopping list",* we are not really interested in the process, but in the result, i.e. the list that exists once it has been written down.

- **Make** can also imply cause:
   Example: *make something happen,*

Take care! It is not always easy to determine if the meaning of a verb is focused on the action or the result of the action.

1.13.2. Do

The most significant uses of **do** in English are:

- as an **auxiliary** used in negative forms of the simple present tense, as in *I don't speak Latin* (see present tenses).

- Just occasionally **do** is used as an auxiliary in affirmative contexts, notably to add weight to the affirmation, or else to add emphasis to an imperative.

> Oh I **don't** like your shirt, but I **do** like your new jacket.
> That music's far too loud! **Do** turn the volume down.

- as a **pro-verb,** used to **avoid repeating** a lexical verb, as in:

> You know more than I **do.**
> I got better marks in the exam than my brother **did**.

- as a **pro-verb** used in questions to **anticipate** the verb that will be used in the answer, as in:

> What are you **doing**? / I'm writing a letter.
> *In this example do anticipates the verb write.*

- as a verb denoting action in a limited number of common expressions.

Common English expressions using do

> To **do** a job / the housework / your homework / the washing up / the
>   shopping   etc.
> To **do** something wrong / right.
> To **do** something very quickly / slowly / clever / stupid / etc.
> To **do** your best / To do well
> To **do** business with someone

There are also some idiomatic uses of do, including a couple of prepositional uses of the verb to do, notably:

> That will **do** meaning *That is enough.*
> To **do without**, as in *There was no bread left, so we had to do without it*
>   *at dinner.*
> To **do up**, as in *The house looked very old, but they did it up and now it*
>   *looks like new.*

1.13.3. Make

The verb *make* usually implies cause or creation. It is used four main ways.

1. As a **causative** verb as in:

> I **made** him tell me all about his vacation in Hawaii.
> The things he said **made** me very angry.

2. As a **standard** verb (a lexical verb) meaning to *create* or *produce* as in:

> Did you **make** that cake yourself?
> I've **made** lunch for everyone.
> They **make** Ford cars in Detroit.
> He doesn't **make** much money working as a barman.

3. In a number of **prepositional** verbs or phrasal verbs (see § 1.18 Prepositional verbs), notably:

> To **make do with** (= to be satisfied by or to manage with)
>   Example: There was no beer, so they *had to make do with* water.
> To **make out** (= to claim, to pretend, or to distinguish)
> To **make up** (= to invent, or to become friends again)
> To **make up for** (= to compensate for)
> To **make it** (= to succeed)
>   Examples: *I made it!!!   or The Lakers made it into the semi-finals*.

4. As a **verb stressing *result*** *or consequence* or the object (the thing that is made) in a number of common expressions. For example, in the expression *to make a statement*, it is the **statement** we are interested in, not the process of making it.

Common English expressions using **make**.

To **make** breakfast / a cup of tea / a cup of coffee / a sandwich ... etc.
To **make** a complaint
To **make** an exception
To **make** an excuse
To **make** a fortune (= to make lots of money)
To **make** friends with
To **make** money
To **make** a mess
To **make** a mistake
To **make** an offer
To **make** peace
To **make** a phone call
To **make** a point
To **make** progress
To **make** a statement
To **make** a success of something
To **make** up one's mind

To make out (to distinguish, to see)
To make up (to put on makeup, to invent, to become friends again)

1.14. Get *and* got

Forms of the verb get

Person	1st / 2nd sing	3rd sing	Plural
Tense	I / you	he, she, etc.	we / you / they
Present.	**get**	**gets**	**get**
Preterit	**got**		
.Past participle	**got** (or **gotten**, USA only)		

1.14.1. Get as a main verb

The verb *to get* is one of the most common verbs in the English language, and for this reason it has a lot of different meanings.

As a main verb, get plays the part of a "**pro-verb**" in the way that "*it*" is a "**pronoun**". Often it is combined with a particle (preposition or adverb); examples of this are treated below. In such cases, **get** is a full verb in its own right, most commonly with the meanings of *acquire, become, cause or arrive*.... but several other meanings are possible (examples 1 - 12 below).

In the **present perfect**, *have got* often functions as a present tense, meaning *have* or *possess* (examples 13 and 14 below).

Get + object + past participle: as in *get it mended* - **get** is used in the meaning of cause (to happen) - (examples 15 - 17 below).

Examples of get as a main verb

1. I'm **getting** a new car tomorrow. (*acquiring, buying*)
2. He **gets** very cross when you ask him personal questions. (*becomes*)
3. I'm **getting** someone to cut the grass. (*finding, employing*)
4. We'll **get** to London at 7.30 pm. (*arrive*)
5. I'm going **to get** top marks in my exam. (*achieve*)
6. I just don't **get** it! (*understand*)
7. If you don't take your pills, you may **get** typhoid. (*catch, acquire*)
8. It's almost six thirty; we really ought **to get going** now. (*start*)
9. I **got** the last two loaves of bread in the shop. (bought, *acquired*)
10. We're **getting** rather cold waiting for you. (*become*)

11. He's just **gotten** a new job. (*found*)
12. Hello! We're early, but we'**ve got** here faster than expected. (*reached, arrived*)
13. He'**s got** two sisters and a brother. (*has, possesses*)
14. He'**s got** three Cadillacs and a Bentley. (*has, possesses*)
15. I'**m getting** a new suit made specially for my wedding.
16. He **got** his photo taken by a famous photographer.
17. **Have** you **got** everything finished?

Has got **or** *has gotten* **in American English?**

Gotten is the normal **past participle** in American English **only** when the verb **get** is used in the present perfect, with the meaning of *become* or *reached* or *acquired.*

American English **does not** use **gotten** in the **present** meaning of *possess* or *has/have*. In British English, **gotten** is not used at all.

He's just **got / gotten** a new job. (*found, acquired*)
Hello! We're early, but **we've got / gotten** here faster than expected.
    (*reached, arrived)*
There's a storm coming; **it's got / gotten** very dark outside. (*become*)
NO! He's **got** / ~~gotten~~ two sisters and a brother. (*has, possesses*)
NO! He's **got** / ~~gotten~~ three Cadillacs and a Tesla. (*has, possesses*)

1.14.2. Phrasal and prepositional verbs with get

Get is the base verb used in a considerable number of phrasal and prepositional verbs in English. Unfortunately there is no way to master and understand them all without learning them either deliberately or through practice.

Here are some of the more common examples:
Two-part verbs: *Get across, get away, get by, get down, get in, get on, get round, get through, get out, get over, get up*

We ought to **get away** by six at the latest. (*depart, leave*)
I'm trying to **get** this **across** simply. (*explain*)
We ought to be able to **get by with** $100. (*manage, succeed*)
Can I **get down**, please.. (*leave the table*)
Get in quickly, it's going to rain very hard. (*go in, enter*)

Peter and Natalia **get on** very well together. (*like each other*)

I can't **get through** this in a week. (*do, finish*)

Get out!. (*Leave, go away!*)

He's **gotten over** COVID-19 quite quickly. (*recovered from*)

I **got round** the problem by using my head. (*avoided, got past*)

I always **get up** late on Sundays. (*get out of bed*)

Three-part verbs: *Get away with, get down to, get on with, get round to*, the meanings should be clear from the examples.

He looks so innocent he could **get away with** murder .

Come on, it's already 8.30, it's time to **get down to** work.

Get on with the job, and stop looking out of the window.

I've got too much work this week, so I don't think I can **get round to** mending your computer too.

1.14.3. **Get** as passive auxiliary

Get with past participle

Get is often used, particularly in colloquial styles, as a passive auxiliary, in place of **be**. (see § 1.11.) As with other forms of the passive, passive sentences with get are mostly intransitive, though get can also be used in **ditransitive** passives (passives with an object) (Examples 6 - 8 below).

1. Sorry I'm late, the plane **got** (was) delayed.
2. My grandfather **got** (was) killed in the war.
3. She's **getting** (being) driven to the ceremony in a big limousine.
4. Survival training includes **getting** (being) dropped in the middle of the desert.
5. We're **getting** (being) picked up at 7.15 tomorrow morning.
6. She **got** (was) given a lovely present by her boyfriend.
7. Everyone **got** (was) clearly told what to do by the team leader.
8. I **got** (was) asked a very difficult question.

1.14.4. **Got to** - modal auxiliary

▶ For information on "got to" as a modal verb, see the following section Modals of obligation § 1.15.1.1.

1.15. Modal verbs of obligation

For purposes of clarity, the term **modal verbs** is used here as a semantic label (i.e. meaning) not as a syntaxic label (i.e. specific verbal features.)

Must, have to, should **and** *ought to*

There are two types of modal verbs of obligation;

1. those that primarily express a **firm obligation** or **necessity** - must and have to
2. those that imply **recommendation** or **moral obligation** - should and ought to.

1.15.1. Firm obligation, etc. - must and have to

The verb must only exists in the *simple present* and *present perfect* forms.

While the present form can express obligation, necessity, certainty or strong probability, the present perfect forms *only* express a strongly felt opinion or supposition. See examples in section 1.15.1.2.

All persons	**Present**	Present perfect
Affirmative	must	**must have**
Negative	*must not, mustn't*	**must not have, mustn't have**

If other tenses are required, the speaker or writer must use forms of the synonymous modal verb "**have to**". This modal auxiliary has all normal tenses, including progressive or continuous forms; these are not common, but need to be used in some cases.

Principal tenses	Present	Present perfect	Past	Future
Affirmative	**has to, have to**	has had to have had to	had to	will have to
Negative *	does not have to, do not have to, doesn't have to don't have to	has not had to have not had to	did not have to didn't have to *	will not have to won't have to
Progressive or continuous	am having to is having to, are having to	has been having to have been having to	was having to were having to	will be having to

* The form "*had not to*" is sometimes used, but it is generally considered to be archaic.

1.15.1.1. *Got to:*

In spoken English, and in the <u>present and preterit forms only</u>, **have to** is often substantiated by the word **got**;
　　For example an alternative to *I have to* is *I've got to*.
► For more on this, see § 1.14 Get and got.

1.15.1.2. *Examples:*

Examples of **modals of obligation** being used to express:

　　　a. Firm <u>obligation</u> or <u>necessity</u>

　　　b. <u>Certainty</u> or strong <u>probability</u>.

　　　c. **Must have** only: <u>supposition</u>

a1) You **must** see a doctor at once!

a2) I **have to** be at school tomorrow at 8 a.m. I have an exam!

a21) I've **got to** be at school tomorrow at .....

a3) You **mustn't** touch that plate, it's too hot.

a4) I **had to** see a doctor, because I felt very sick.

a5) I **had to** break the window! I lost my key!

a6) The manager isn't here, he**'s had to** go to Miami on urgent business.

a7) Tomorrow the President **will have to** open the new building.

a8) She**'s having to** move because she can't stand the noise.

a9) I**'m having to** take out this detonator very slowly, to avoid an
　　　　　explosion.

a10) Oh you're so kind! You **didn't have to** do it as well as that!

b1) He **must** be over eighty, he was born in 1938.

b2) If my brother's not in Chicago, he **has to** be in New York.

b3) I've got all the right answers, I **must** be one of the winners!

b4) If I remember correctly, it **has to** be here.

c1) I can't find my laptop, I **must have** left it in the train.

c2) If they're out, they **mustn't have** heard the news.

Take care!
Take care to distinguish correctly between "**had to**" and "**must have**":

> *They **had to** go to Washington.*
>   = They were obliged to go to Washington.
> *They **must have** gone to Washington.*
>   = In my opinion, they have certainly gone to Washington.

▶ Other uses of the verb have: see § 1.12 The verb to have.

1.15.2. Recommendation or moral obligation - Should and ought to

The verb **should** only exists in the simple present, and present perfect forms.

Forms of should

All persons	Present	Present perfect
Affirmative	should	should have
Negative	should not, shouldn't	should not have, shouldn't have

The verb **ought to** only exists in simple present and present perfect forms.

Forms of ought to

All persons	Present	Present perfect
Affirmative	ought to	ought to have
Negative	ought not to, oughtn't to	ought not to have, oughtn't to have

Should and ought to are more or less synonymous.

Examples

a1) You **should** stop smoking (= You ought to stop smoking.)
a2) It's raining hard, the children **ought to** come indoors.
a3) I didn't know you were married! You **ought to have** told me
a4) If you'd wanted to succeed, you **should have** worked harder at
       school.
a5) This pullover's got holes in it, I **should** get a new one.
a6) This pullover's got holes in it, I **ought to** get a new one.
a7) That's awful! You really **oughtn't to have** done that, you know!

1.16. Modal verbs of ability

Modal verbs of ability are used to express two different types of ability:

Open possibility, generally expressed by forms of **can**,

Authority or potential ability, usually expressed by forms of **may**.

These two verbs are followed by the infinitive without *to*.

1.16.1. Open possibility - can and be able to

The verb can only exists in the simple present, simple past and present perfect forms.

All persons	**Present**	Past	Present perfect
Affirmative	**can**	**could**	**can have** + participle
Negative	can not, cannot, can't	could not, couldn't	cannot have

If other tenses are required, the speaker or writer must use forms of the synonymous modal verb "**be able to**". This modal auxiliary has all necessary tenses, as it is in reality just the verb **to be** followed by the adjective **able**.

The verb **be able to** is **not used** in progressive or continuous tenses, but the present participle / gerund *being able to* is sometimes used (example a9 below).

Sample tenses	**Present**	Present perfect	Past	Future
Affirmative:	am able to, are able to is able to	has been able to have been able to	was able to were able to	will be able to
Negative; sample forms	am not able to , am unable to	has not been able to has been unable to	was not able to was unable to	will not be able to will be unable to

Can and **able to** are used to express:

- a. Physical or potential **ability.** (Examples a1 – a8)

- b. **Authority** to do something (by confusion with **may**) – (Examples b1 and b2)
- c. **Can** only: in the present perfect, a past possibility. (Example c1) This is particularly common with negative clauses.

Examples

> a1) I **can** speak three different languages, English, French and Spanish.
> a2) He **can't** open the door, it's stuck.
> a3) **I'm able to** speak three languages, German, English and Russian.
> a4) He**'s unable to** get into his car, he's lost the key.
> a5) When I lived in New York, I **could** walk to work in five minutes.
> a6) If you lose the key, you **won't be able to** get into your apartment.
> a7) I **haven't been able to** finish the job, it's too difficult.
> a8) In spite long discussions, they **were unable to** reach an agreement.
> a9) **Being able to** speak English well is a useful skill.
> b1) The police officer says we **can** go in now.
> b2) **Can** we please sit down!
> c1)   They **cannot have** seen the warning sign.....

Take care !

Be careful to distinguish correctly between "**could not**" and "**cannot have**".

> *They **could not see** the warning sign*
> = They **were unable to see it**, for example, because it was hidden.
> *They **cannot have seen** the warning sign.....*
> = They **must have not seen it**, even though it was there and visible.

1.16.2. Potential possibility or authority
- may and might

The verb **may** only exists in the simple present, past and present perfect forms. The simple past form of **may** is **might**. *Might* is also used in its own right as a present tense modal.

Forms of may

All persons	**Present**	Past	Present perfect
Affirmative	**may**	**might**	**may have**
Negative	may not	might not	may not have

Forms of might

All persons	**Present**	Past	Present perfect
Affirmative	**might**	**might**	**might have**
Negative	might not	might not	*might not have*

Uses of may and might

- a) The modal **may** is used to imply <u>potentiality</u> (*limited possibility*) or <u>authority</u> to do something. Using the modal **may** is frequently the same as qualifying a statement with the word **perhaps**. Its past form **might** is most commonly found in dependent clauses, notably in reported speech. **Note** that a synonym of **perhaps** is **maybe**.... which is of course composed of the words *may* and *be*. (Examples a1 – a41).

- b) Used in the present perfect form (may + have + past participle), **may** is also used to express <u>possibility</u> **that occurred in a relative past** (something that *perhaps* occurred), i.e. in past time with relation to the present or to some other moment.

- c) **Might** is also used to imply <u>remote possibility</u>, i.e. something that *could just be possible*. In this sense, it is often combined with **be able to**.

- d) Used in the present perfect (might + have + past participle), **might** is also used to express a <u>hypothetical possibility</u> (affirmative or negative) **in the past**. This is particularly common in type 3 conditional clauses.

- e) **Might** and **may** can both be used to imply politeness or sarcasm.

Examples

<table>
<tr><td>a1)</td><td>We **may** (perhaps) go to England next year, if we have enough money.</td></tr>
<tr><td>a2)</td><td>But of course, we **may** not be able to afford it.</td></tr>
<tr><td>a3)</td><td>The policeman said "You **may** go now".</td></tr>
<tr><td>a31)</td><td>The policeman told me I **might** go.</td></tr>
<tr><td>a4)</td><td>I **may not** be able to get home on time.</td></tr>
<tr><td>a41)</td><td>She said she **might not** be able to get home on time.</td></tr>
<tr><td>b1)</td><td>I **may have** left my cellphone on the plane.</td></tr>
<tr><td>b2)</td><td>It's five o'clock; they **may have** finished by now.</td></tr>
<tr><td>b3)</td><td>I **may have** seen something very important.</td></tr>
<tr><td>c1)</td><td>I **might** find a job if I'm lucky.</td></tr>
<tr><td>c2)</td><td>I think they'll get the contract, but they **might** not.</td></tr>
<tr><td>c3)</td><td>I **might** be able to get tickets for the show tonight, it's just possible!</td></tr>
<tr><td>d1)</td><td>You're very lucky to be alive; you **might have** died!</td></tr>
<tr><td>d2)</td><td>I'm afraid that someone **might have** heard us.</td></tr>
<tr><td>d3)</td><td>I **might have** won if I'd run just a little bit faster.</td></tr>
<tr><td>d4)</td><td>You **might not have** broken it if you'd been more careful.</td></tr>
<tr><td>e1)</td><td>(Please) **may** I say how happy I am to be here!</td></tr>
<tr><td>e2)</td><td>**Might** I ask what you are doing?</td></tr>
</table>

1.17. Verbs of enabling and obligation

Enablement permission prevention and causation

Verbs of enablement and obligation, or causative verbs, often cause problems for students. In English, they have some rather particular structures that may not correspond to structures in other languages. Here are the basic rules, to help you master these important verbs.

1.17.1. Verbs of obligation or authority:

allow, ask, authorize, instruct, invite, leave, oblige, permit, require, tell, want etc.

After these verbs, **the second verb is in the infinitive with to.**

> He **told** me **to hurry.**
> They **allowed** us **to leave** the room.
> The man **instructed** me **to come** down.
> The police **required** me **to give** a blood sample.
> I **want** you **to know** I love you.

N.B. With all these verbs, the subordinate clause must be introduced by a **subject**, which is also the object of the main clause: for example, **we cannot say**:

> ** The man **permitted to open** the doors **
>   ** I **told not to do** that **

All the verbs listed can be easily used in the passive except **want**.

> The singer **was told t**o come down.
> He **was invited** to give a concert.
> She **was forbidden** to leave the room.
> I **was required** to fill in a form.
> They **were asked** to sit down.

1.17.2. Verbs of prevention:

1. Stop, prevent, hinder :

These verbs are followed by **"from"** and an *-ing* structure. The word "from" is essential with **hinder**, optional with **stop** and **prevent**.

He **hindered** us from starting in time.
He **stopped** me (from) falling in the hole.
They **prevented** me (from) going out.

Stop is not usually used in the passive, but **hinder** and **prevent** easily accept passive structures:

The hoodlums **were prevented from** making trouble.
We **were hindered** by the bad weather.

2. Forbid

The verb **forbid** is followed by a **full infinitive** with *to*, just like verbs of obligation above. It can also be used in the passive.

I'm going to **forbid** the children to stay out after 9 o'clock.
They **were forbidden** to stay out after nine o'clock at night.

1.17.3. Causative verbs - verbs of direct authority:

1. let, make, have, tell.

Of these verbs, only **let** can be used as a consecutive verb, i.e. followed directly by a second verb. **Make have** and **tell** must always be followed by a noun or pronoun complement; with **make** & **have** the second verb is in the short infinitive **without** *to*; *tell* is followed by a full infinitive **with to.**

I **told** you **to let** go!
I **let** him **do** it.
He **made** me **sit** down.
Have him **tell** you what he saw!

Of these verbs, only one can be used in the passive, **make**.

I **was made** to take off my skates.

Don't confuse **let** and **leave**: when followed by an object and a subsidiary clause, **leave** means *abandon, quit.*

We **left** him **to** get on with his work. (i.e. *we went away*)
        does not mean the same as
We **let** him get on with his work (i.e. *we allowed him to....*)

2. Get

With this verb, the second verb form is the full infinitive with *to.*

I **got** the people **to** read the instructions very carefully.

(▶ For more on **got**, see § 1.14.1)

1.18. Phrasal and prepositional verbs

Phrasal verbs, also called **particle verbs**, are reputed to be the hardest point of English grammar to master. **Why** does one say:

> I **looked it up** on the Internet,   *but*   I **looked for it** on the Internet **?**

To answer this question, we first need to understand that **with transitive verbs** there are two different verb+particle combinations in English; on the one hand there are **phrasal verbs**; on the other hand **prepositional verbs.**

One big problem here is that many guides to English use the expression "*phrasal verb*" indiscriminately to describe every situation in which a verb is followed by a preposition or a particle. To avoid this problem, let's start by defining some terms.

◆ A **phrasal verb** (**or particle verb)** is a verb that combines with a particle. Particles are prepositions or adverbs, depending on the circumstances: for example the adverb *over* is the particle in *Why don't you come **over** tonight !*

◆ A **prepositional verb** is a *verb whose meaning is defined or determined by the preposition that follows it.*

The next difficulty is that unfortunately it may seem impossible to distinguish between a **phrasal verb** and a **prepositional verb**. These verbs may be used transitively in the same way in active statements when they are followed by a noun. It is only when we replace the noun with a pronoun, or try to put the sentence into the passive, that the differences become more clear, as the following examples show.

With **nouns as objects**	With **pronoun objects**	(Passive - if possible)
The car **ran over** the dog	The **car** ran it over	The dog **was run over** by the car.
The soldiers **ran** <u>over the road</u>	The soldiers ran <u>over it.</u>	Improbable.
The editor quickly **looked through** the new book	He quickly looked it through	It **was** quickly **looked through** by the editor.
We **looked** <u>through the window</u> at the garden.	We looked <u>through it</u> into at the garden.	Impossible
I **got off** all the dirty marks.	I got them all off	All the dirty marks **were got off** by me. (Improbable)
I **got** <u>off the Greyhound</u> at Boston.	I got <u>off it</u> at Boston	Impossible

▶ The examples on the yellow lines use phrasal verbs (or particle verbs). The preposition is an **integral part of the verb**, defining its meaning.

▶ The examples on the blue lines either use prepositional verbs, where the preposition **determines the meaning** of the verb, but is part of the **adverb phrase** following the verb; or they are are just a verb followed by a preposition.

 Fortunately, verbs like those in the examples above, which can be *either* phrasal or prepositional verbs, are uncommon. With the vast majority of verbs, there is no choice. The verb is *either* a phrasal verb *or* a prepositional verb.

The problem is to know which. Why is *look up* a phrasal verb but *look for* a prepositional verb? That is a very difficult question to answer.

Nevertheless recognising that there are two different types of {verb+preposition} structure should start to make things a bit easier…. but not completely clear. The real key to understanding the differences between phrasal verbs and prepositional verbs is the principle of separability.

1.18.1. Separable or inseparable?

The principle of **separability** applies to **transitive** verbs only (verbs which can be followed by an object). Can a transitive verb such as *make* and its particle such as *up* be separated by a direct object ?

 If the answer is yes, it is separable, and is a phrasal verb.

 If the answer is no, it is inseparable, and is a prepositional verb.

The key differences between separable verbs and inseparable verbs are:

- **Separable** verbs are all transitive. They can be separated only by a **direct object**, but **not** normally by adverbs or adverb phrases.
- **Inseparable verbs,** which may be transitive or intransitive, can occasionally be separated by adverbs or adverb phrases, but **not** by their direct object.

	Transitive	Intransitive
Phrasal verbs	**Separable** *I looked the word **up.** or I looked **up** the word in the dictionary.*	**Inseparable** *Please sit down.*
Prepositional verbs	**Inseparable** *I **looked** (in vain) **for** the word.*	

1.18.2. Transitive verbs

1.18.2.1. Almost all *transitive phrasal verbs* are *separable.*

This means that a **noun object** may come between the verb and the particle, and a **pronoun object** must come between the verb and the particle. There are hundreds of separable phrasal verbs in English. The table below shows the principal root verbs from which separable phrasal verbs can be created, and the principal particles that are used to create them.

Principal roots of separable verbs	Sample pronoun object	Main particles used
break, bring, call, check, cut, give, hold, keep, leave, let, look, make, put, run, set, take, think, turn, work, write	it	down, in, over, off, on, out, over, round, through, up
Example: Let me check **it out**.		

Almost all combinations of these verbs with the particles indicated will be separable. Note that each root verb will only combine with **certain** particles, **not** all of them.

Transitive phrasal verbs : examples in different contexts

With noun objects	With pronoun objects	(Passive if possible)
The referee **broke up** (=*stopped*) the fight immediately. **or:** The referee **broke** the fight **up** immediately.	He **broke** it **up** immediately.	The fight was immediately **broken up** by the referee.
The old lady made out (=*wrote*) the cheque very slowly. **or:** The old lady **made** the cheque **out** very slowly.	She **made** it **out** very slowly.	The cheque was **made out** by the old lady very slowly.
He **took up** (=*started*) golf when he retired. **or:** He **took** golf up when he retired.	He **took** it **up** when he retired.	*improbable*
The robbers **set off** (=*started*) the alarm as they entered the bank. **or:** The robbers **set** the alarm **off** as they entered the bank.	They **set** it **off** as they entered the bank.	The alarm was **set off** as the robbers entered the bank.
The men managed to **put out** (=*extinguish*) the fire by themselves. **or:** The men managed to **put** the fire **out** by themselves	They managed to **put** it **out** by themselves.	The fire was **put out** by the men, by themselves.

1.18.2.2. Transitive prepositional verbs are inseparable

General features of prepositional verbs

1. The preposition defines or limits the meaning of the verb, and is an <u>essential link</u> between the verb and its stated or implied object. Compare: *pay me* or *pay a bill* with **pay for** *lunch.*

2. Often, prepositions serve to form a *transitive* **verb** from an *intransitive* **root verb: Examples:** *look / look at / look for - wait / wait for - come / come through.*

3. *With prepositional verbs* the direct object **must** follow the {verb+particle} unit. It makes no difference whether the object is a pronoun or a noun.

Prepositional verbs can be formed from a large number of root verbs, and an almost full range of prepositions.

Sample root verbs	Main prepositions used	Sample object
go, fall, look, think; agree, believe, are, consist, insist, laugh, look, pay, result, wait, work…. *etc.*	About, after, at, before, by, for, from, on, to, **down, in, over, of, off, on, out, round, through, up,** without	**it**
Example: We **went** (**quickly**) **through** it last night.		

Note that this list contains verbs and particles that are *also* used in transitive phrasal verbs, plus some additional prepositions , notably : *by, for, on,* and *without*.

Transitive prepositional verbs *- examples in different contexts*

With **noun objects**	With **pronoun objects**	Passive
They **came through** (=*passed*) their exam very well.	They **came through** it very well	*Improbable*
We're **depending on** your support, totally.	We're totally **depending on** it.	Your support is being **depended on**. (possible but unlikely)
The students **looked intently at** (= *studying*) the text	They **looked intently at** it , **or** They **looked at** it **intently**.	

1.18.3. Intransitive verbs

1.18.3.1 Intransitive verbs with particles are inseparable.

With **intransitive verbs** there is no distinction between phrasal and prepositional verbs. All intransitive verbs with particles are **inseparable**.

Principal root verbs	**Main particles** used
come, do, fall, go, sit; break, bring, call, check, cut, give, hold, keep, leave, let, look, make, put, run, set, take, think, turn, work, write	About, after, at, before, by, for, from, on, to, **down, in, over, off, on, out, round, through, up,** without
Example: Please sit down.	

- **Intransitive verbs** do not have a direct object, so the {verb+particle} unit of an intransitive verb with a particle will by definition be unbroken.
- In **intransitive verbs**, the particle either narrows the sense of the verb (as in *sit down*), or else creates an idiomatic meaning which is different from that of the root verb (as in *shut up*).

Here are a few examples of intransitive verbs:

Flight UA04 to New York will **take off** at 12.33.
Several students **showed up** late.
Covid-19 first **broke out** in China in 2019
Tomorrow morning, we all have to **get up** at 5.30.
Once the President had taken his place, the guests all **sat** *quietly* **down**.

1.18.4. Special cases and exceptions

1.18.3.1 General

Most verbs follow the rules outlined above; some do not. As with so many rules, there are exceptions. The most prolific exceptions are with the verb *get* (see below), but there are also a number of verbs, for example with *into* or *round,* that do not reflect the general rules. We can say *turn into* something, or *turn something into…* but the meanings are different. We say to *look round a house,* but to *take something round to someone's house.* Examples like these just have to be learned.

1.18.3.1 Verbs using get

The verb *get* is used in many phrasal and prepositional verbs. Some words, such as *get off,* are phrasal verbs or prepositional verbs according context. For more details see §1.14.2.

1.8.3.2 *Inseparable phrasal-prepositional verbs*

Double particle verbs, or phrasal-prepositional verbs, are mostly prepositional verbs in which the root verb is actually a phrasal verb; so in reality, the structure of these verbs is {phrasal-verb} + preposition. Like simple prepositional verbs, transitive phrasal-prepositional verbs are **inseparable**.

Once this is understood usage should not be hard to follow.

Using **nouns**	Using **pronoun objects**	(Passive)
Everyone looked forward to the event.	Everyone looked forward to it.	It was looked forward to by everyone.
The prisoners broke out of their cells.	They broke out of them.	The cells were broken out of.
We made up for lost time.	We made up for it.	Lost time was made up (for) (as + *explanation*).
The airline did away with tickets	The airline did away with them	Tickets were done away with by the airline.

1.19. Irregular verbs

English has over 150 fairly common irregular verbs. Some of these have the same form in the preterit and the past participle, for example:

Present	**Simple past (preterit)**	**Past participle**
bet	bet (or betted)	bet (or betted)
bid	bid (or bade)	bid
burst	burst	burst

Most have forms in which the preterit and past participle forms are different, for example:

arise	arose	arisen
bear	bore	born
beat	beat	beaten
begin	began	begun
fly	flew	flown

For full lists, see **Irregular verb lists** on Linguapress online grammar.

2. The noun phrase

2.1. Nouns : what is a noun?

A **noun** is a lexical word that represents an **entity** (person, creature, object), a **substance**, a **process** (action, evolution) or an **abstraction** (idea, concept).

Nouns representing named person/s, entity, or place are called **proper** nouns and are **C**apitalized. Other nouns are known as or **common** nouns.

2.1.1. The classification of nouns

Every noun can be classified in three different ways.
Proper or common?   **Concrete or abstract?**   **Count or non-count?**

- **Proper nouns:** Nouns representing a named person entity, or place are called **proper** nouns and are **C**apitalized. We also call them "names". **Examples**: *Shakespeare, Philadelphia, India, Mount Rushmore, the Titanic, the Olympics, Catholicism, Islam, Google, Gandalf.* They are usually concrete and uncountable. Other nouns are known as or **common** nouns.

- **Common nouns:** Nouns that denote entities or substances (even invisible or intangible substances such as air) are called **concrete nouns**; nouns denoting abstractions or processes are called **abstract nouns**.

- **Common nouns** designating items or abstractions that can be counted are known as **count nouns** (or *countable nouns*), and have both singular and plural forms. Nouns designating generalizations or substances are called **non-count nouns** (or *uncountable nouns*) and are normally only used in the singular.

- Almost all non-count nouns **can** also be <u>used as</u> count nouns in certain circumstances, though most often only in the singular. The distinction between count and non-count nouns is fundamental, as they are not used in the same way.

- ▶ For more on this see count and non-count nouns (§ 2.3.)

Common nouns	Count	Non-count
Concrete	car, cat, ball, man, table, engine, class, road, aeroplane,	water, potassium, cement, air, oil, whisky, concrete
Abstract	idea, noun, attitude, name, song, thought, opinion, victory, quantity, length, kilometer	patience, suspense, life, philosophy, music, , work, economics

Examples of non-count nouns being used as count nouns in defined circumstances:

Whisky is an alcoholic drink. This bar has **fifteen different** whiskies.
Work can be interesting, but **this** work I'm doing is very boring.
Love is all you need; and John had **three** loves, his wife, his kids and his car.
I love music, but I particularly love **the** music of Mozart.

While the plural forms *whiskies*, *works* and *loves* are all possible, such plural forms are uncommon. Generally speaking, non-count abstract nouns, for example *suspense, patience* or *music*, cannot be used in the plural.

2.1.2. Nouns and gender

In English, nouns can either be masculine (referring to men or more generally to male creatures), feminine (referring to women, or more generally to female creatures), or neutral (referring to objects, substances, processes or abstractions.)

Contrary to some other European languages, the *gender* of a noun is **not** reflected in the article or adjective that is linked to it.

Thus one says: a man, a lady, a cat, a decision, this man, this lady

On the other hand, the gender of a noun is reflected in the **third person singular** in **personal pronouns** and in **possessive pronouns and adjectives** relating to it. Thus

I saw **the boy** > becomes I saw **him**.
I saw **the girl** > becomes I saw **her**.
I saw **the cat** > becomes I saw **it**.
This is **Mark's** computer > becomes This is **his** computer
This is **Mary's** computer > becomes This is **her** computer.

For more details see below: Articles, Pronouns, and Possessives.

2.1.3. The formation of nouns

Many nouns represent primary entities; these are **root nouns** such as:

Apple, Boot, Child, Dog, Egg, Finger, Giraffe, Hand, Island......

There are **no rules** that govern the form of a root noun.

Other nouns, known as **derived nouns**, are formed from verbs, adjectives or from other nouns.

  The formation of derived nouns in English is very easy. This is one of the strengths of the English language! Most frequently, derived nouns are formed from a **root** (not necessarily another existing word, but a "lexeme", a unit of lexical meaning) to which is added a prefix or a suffix. Most endings imply a specific or general meaning.

Here are the most common suffixed used to form nouns in English:
-ion , -ence, -ness, -ment, -ity, -ics, -ing .

Examples

Action, nation, inflation, discussion - with ***-ion***
Patience, maintenance, conscience - with ***(i)ence*** or -***(i)ance***
Madness, emptiness, loneliness, greatness - with ***-ness***
Parliament, instrument, apartment, containment, - with **-ment**
Community, commodity, validity, - with ***-ity***
Physics, economics, analytics, statistics, logistics - with ***-ics***
Farming, marketing, beginning, ending, with ***-ing***

2.1.4. Nouns in the plural

Pluralizing nouns in English is very simple. With just a few exceptions, the plural of all English nouns is formed by adding the letter "**s**".

Exceptions to the general principle:

Nouns in s, sh, ss, ch or z,

When the singular of an English noun ends in **s, sh, ss, ch** or **z**, the plural is normally formed by adding **–es.**

Examples: Bus > buses, Bush > bushes, Match > matches, Mass > masses, Buzz > buzzes,

With some words ending in **s**, the plural and singular are identical.
Examples: A series > two series, a means > two means > a species > two species.

Nouns ending in -f.

With **some** (but not all) nouns ending in a single **-f ,** the plural is formed by replacing the final **-f** by **-ves**.

Examples: Half >halves, hoof > hooves, thief > thieves but Roof > roofs, belief > beliefs
The same goes for words ending in **-fe** (or -ef).
Examples: Knife >knives, life > lives, thief > thieves.

Words ending in -is

With words like analysis, hypothesis, the plural is formed by replacing the final **-is** by **-es**, **Examples**: analysis > analyses, hypothesis > hypotheses, crisis > crises etc.

Some words derived directly or supposedly from Latin or Greek

In some cases, the original Latin or Greek ending is used.
Cactus > cacti, Medium > media, nucleus > nuclei, criterion > criteria, stimulus > stimuli etc.

A few irregular nouns

A very small number of common English nouns have irregular plurals. Man > men , woman > women , child> children, mouse > mice, foot> feet, tooth > teeth …

Animals and fish

For some animals, some birds, and a lot of fish (including the word **fish**), the plural is - or may be - **the same** as the singular.

A bison > two bison, a deer > two deer(s), a fish > two fish, a perch > two perch, a salmon > two salmon, a sheep > two sheep, a grouse > two grouse etc.

Most other animals and birds have regular plurals: two horses, two cats, two dogs, two pigs, two pigeons, two eagles etc.

Nouns of nationality in the plural

Nouns of nationality ending in **–sh -ch -ese** or **-ss** do not take any plural ending; they are **invariable**. Other nouns of nationality obey the general rules for plurals.

Examples: The English, the Scottish, the Spanish, the French, the Dutch, the Swiss, the Portuguese, the Chinese, the Japanese, the Lebanese....

But: The Americans, the Australians, the Finns, the Swedes, the Russians, the Poles, the Brazilians, the Serbs, the Greeks, the Moroccans, the Afghans, the Pakistanis, etc.

2.1.5. Collective nouns - singular or plural?

Collective nouns, or **group** nouns, are nouns such as **family, government, class** or **committee**, which refer to groups of people or things.

In **American English**, these are generally considered as singular nouns, while in British English they are commonly used as if they were plurals,

Examples: in this example, both alternatives are acceptable:

> The administration **has** decided to increase security measures.
> The government **have** decided to increase security measures.

> The whole class **is** going to take the test again *may sound strange to a British English speaker, who will prefer*
> The whole class **are** going to take the test again.

because in this case, it is clear that each student of the class will be taking the test again *individually*. At least, that is what the teachers intend should happen!

Sometimes a plural is essential, even in American English, for example:

> My family **are** immigrants.

We could not possibly say

> ~~My family is immigrants~~   or (even worse!) ~~My family is an immigrant~~.

In this case, it is **context** that requires a plural verb. In other cases, a singular verb will be possible:

> My whole family is /are coming to see me this weekend.

2.1.5.1. What is the rule?

In modern **American** usage, the accepted rule follows grammatical (syntaxic) logic, which is to use a singular verb with collective nouns, because these nouns are grammatically singular – though even in the USA this is not always the case.

In British English, the rule is to follow semantic logic, the logic of meaning, so if the **collective unit** - *family, government, committee, club, class* or whatever is being treated as a **single** entity, doing things **collectively**, then we will usually put the verb into the **singular**.

If, on the other hand, the collective unit is being seen as a **group** of **individuals**, each doing things as an **individual**, then we tend to use a **plural**. So …

> The committee **has** decided .... gives the impression that the committee has made a **unanimous** decision.
> The committee **have** decided .... gives the impression that the members of the committee have all (or mostly) decided of their own **individual** free will.

A special case

> The word **police** is **always** used in the plural. We cannot say: ~~the police is.....~~

2.1.5.2. Collective proper nouns (names)

Corporate names, like **Google** or **Facebook** or **Apple**, are a specific type of collective noun. They are used in the same way as the common nouns shown in the examples above, sometimes as singulars, sometimes as plurals.

> We found out today that Google **are** backing up their Location API
> *(Washington Post, May 2008)*
>
> So Google **is** good and bad in one sentence for Donald Trump
> *(Washington Post, Sept 2016)*

And here are two sentences from the same writer in the same article published in the *Guardian* newspaper in England in Nov. 2011

> Microsoft **is** investing massively .... but Microsoft **are** still selling copies of Word.

Take care! *Agreement*

When a collective noun is used as a **singular**, the pronouns used to refer back to is must be *it / its.*   When a collective noun is used as a **plural**, the pronouns used to refer back to is must be *they / them / their.*

Examples

> In **its** monthly report, the committee **says** that the situation is getting better.
> In **their** monthly report, the committee **say** that the situation is getting better.

2.1.5.3. List of important collective nouns

There are at least 100 nouns that can be used as collective nouns, but only a small number of them are commonly used, and need to be remembered; here are twenty of the most important:

administration army audience class club committee company congregation corporation council family firm group jury majority minority parliament public police school team

2.2. Types of noun phrase

A **noun phrase** or **noun group** is a group of words describing or qualifying the noun or pronoun that is the key element in the group. Noun groups can vary in size from a single letter, the pronoun *I*, to a long complex rambling phrase with dependent clauses.

Here are the six essential structures, with examples.

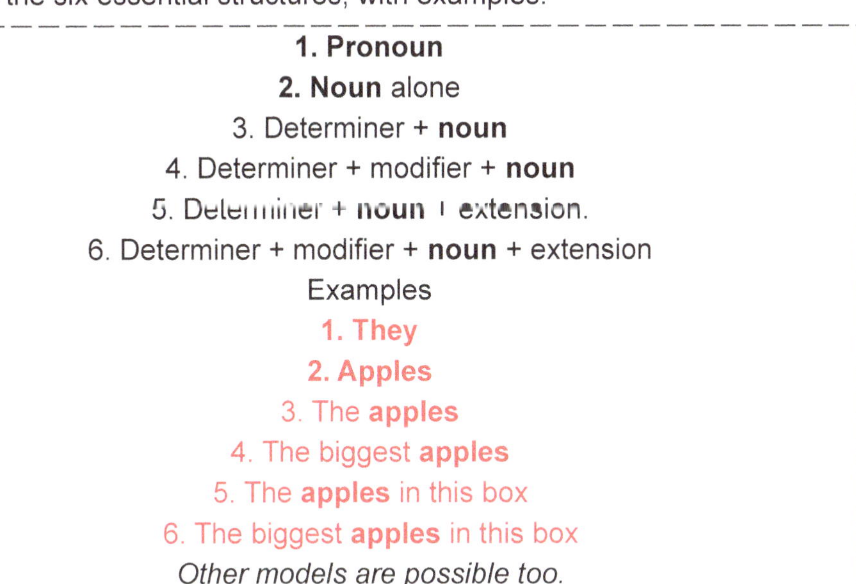

Two simple "rules" govern the use of the noun phrase in English.

2.2.1. Most noun phrases consist of at least two elements

Unless a noun is used in a generalising sense (see articles), or is just a pronoun, a noun phrase consists of at least the following elements: a **determiner** and a **noun**.

A **determiner** is one of the following: an **article** (*the, a, an, some, any*),

- a **quantifier** (*no, few, a few, many, etc.*),
- a **possessive** (*my, your, whose, the man's, etc.*),
- a **demonstrative** (*this, that, these, those*),
- a **numeral** (*one, two, three etc.*)
- or a **question word** (*which, whose, how many, etc.*).

Except in some very rare cases, a noun can only be preceded by **ONE** determiner:

Examples: the man, some women, a few dogs, your horse, the man's horse* , that car, whose money, how many bottles?

*   In the example, **the man's horse*** there appear to be two determiners before **horse**, but in fact there is only one: the determiner before **horse** is "**the man**", in which the article *the* is the determiner of the word **man**.

2.2.2. Many noun phrases also include "modifiers"

There are five essential types of modifier:

A **modifier** can be an **adjective, an adjectival phrase**, a **secondary noun**, a prepositional phrase or a relative clause.
The principal noun in a noun group is called the **head noun**.

1. **Adjectives** are normally placed before the head noun: as in **the Great Gatsby**   (▶ See § 2.9. Adjective order)

2. **Adjective phrases** usually come before the head noun: as in:
    a **black-and-white striped** vest
    a **rather tight-fitting** dress

3. **Secondary nouns** behave exactly like adjectives, and come before the head noun:
    a **beer** glass, the **police** inspector, a **London** bus

4. **Prepositional phrases** and …

5. … relative clauses follow the head noun, as in:
    the students **in our class**   *or* the girl who gave me her phone-number.

Put all this together, and we get a **complex noun group**, such as:

> *The* **nice old-fashioned** **police** **inspector** **with white hair,** who was drinking his beer, *was Mr. Morse.*

2.2.3. Some common exceptions

Sometimes an adjective or an adjectival phrase will follow the noun, or appear to do so. There are three cases that need to be noted:

A very few adjectives always follow the noun: **concerned** (in the sense of "being talked about"), and **involved** (in the sense of "participating", or "being present") are the two common ones.

Other participial adjectives (such as **left, remaining, missing**) appear to be used as adjectives that follow the noun; in reality, they are elliptical forms of a relative clause that has become reduced to a single word.

Adjectives follow the noun when the adjectives themselves are post-modified (defined) by a following phrase.

Examples.
There's been an outbreak of flu, but there are only fifteen people
   concerned.
After the fight, the police arrested the men involved.
Oh look! there is only one chocolate left!!
We can't go yet!! There are still three people missing.
There was a crowd bigger than last year.
   Note that in this case, we could also say:
There was a bigger crowd than last year.
   But not
There was a ~~bigger than~~ last year crowd.

For more examples see § 2.9.3.1 Attributive adjectives

2.3. Count nouns and non-count nouns

In English, as in many other languages, nouns are divided into two categories, known as **"count nouns"** and **"non-count nouns"**. It is important to distinguish between these two groups.

2.3.1. Count nouns

Sometimes called "countable nouns" , these are nouns that refer to things that can be multiplied or counted, for example:

- one man, two trees, three things, four faces, five films, six shops, seven sisters, and so on.

2.3.2. Non-count nouns

These are nouns that refer to generalisations, abstractions, concepts or substances, things that cannot be put in the plural; for example.

- water, oxygen, eternity, psychology, anger, politics, heat, alcohol.... and so on.

So far, so good! That is relatively simple to follow. **Concrete** objects and items can be counted, **concepts** and **abstractions** cannot. Unfortunately, this easy distinction does not take into account all nouns.

The Problem:

> The problem is that there are a lot of nouns that are *either* **count nouns** *or* **non-count nouns** , depending on the circumstances.

2.3.3. Usage

Count nouns and **non-count** nouns are not used in the same way. Most importantly there are the questions of **determiners** or articles (*the, a an, some* and *any,* etc.) and **quantifiers**. The essential rules are not complicated:

> **RULE 1 ▶**
>
> **Count nouns <u>must</u>** have a determiner of some kind in the singular. **In the plural,** count nouns require a determiner if they are used with a restricted value, no determiner if they are used as generalisations.

Examples in the singular

You can say a table, this table, my table, one table, etc. but never just "table".

Examples in the plural

You say "tables" (or "all tables") if you mean *all tables in general,* but "the tables" or "these tables", etc., if you are referring to just *certain tables,* but <u>not</u> *all tables*.

Examples in context:

> Usually, tables have flat surfaces, but **the** tables in this café don't.
> Trucks are big vehicles, but **the** trucks in the USA are enormous.

> **RULE 2 ▶**
>
> **Non-count** **nouns** do not have a determiner in the singular. They are **not used in the plural**

Example: Oxygen is essential for life.

In cases where non-count nouns are used with a determiner, this is because they are being used with a restricted or count value.

For example: **This** oxygen is contaminated.

2.3.4. Problem: nouns that are either count nouns or non count nouns

There are a lot of nouns that are *either* **count nouns** *or* **non-count nouns**, depending on the circumstances.

In their **non-count** form or value, they are generalisations, in their **count noun** form or value their meaning is restricted or slightly different. Look at these examples:

> We all like **beer**, so let's order **three beers**.
> **Air** is vital for life, but **the air** in this room is very unpleasant.
> Radiators should produce **heat**, but **the heat** from that radiator is minimal!
> **Philosophy** is complicated, specially when there are **several different philosophies** about the same situation.

In the examples above, the first time the noun is used with a **non-count** generalising value, beer, air, heat, philosophy.

However the second time these nouns are used they have the restricted value of **count nouns**: for this reason, they must be introduced by a determiner; in the examples, the determiners are a numeral (*three*), two articles (*the*) and two demonstrative determiners (*this* and *that*).

three beers, the air in this room, the heat from that radiator, several different philosophies.

The fact that some nouns can have either a non-count value or a count value does not always mean that we can actually count them! **Many abstractions** cannot be put in the plural; for example

> We **could never** say ~~There are two different airs in these two rooms~~.
> we **cannot** say ~~musics~~ or ~~patiences~~
> though as the examples show, we can say *several different philosophies.*

It is **context** that will usually indicate whether a noun is a **count noun** or a **non-count** noun.

2.3.5. Quantifiers with count and non-count nouns

The choice of certain quantifiers (▶ see § 2.6.) such as *much / many, few / little, some* and *any* depends on whether a noun is a **count noun** or a **non-count** noun.

With **count nouns** in the **plural**, the quantifiers to use are *many, few / a few,* and *some**. Obviously, quantifiers cannot be used with **count nouns** in the singular.

Many people speak English.

Few animals escaped from the forest fire.

A few animals escaped from the forest fire. (*This does not mean the same!*)

The old man was found by **some children**.

**Some* is replaced by *any* in negative and interrogative contexts.

With **non-count** nouns in the singular, the quantifiers to use are *much, little / a little,* and *any*. And remember, **non-count** nouns cannot be used in the plural!

There wasn't **much water** left.

There was **little food** left in the house. (*Meaning* not much food)

There was **a little food** left in the house. (*Meaning* a small amount of food)

There wasn't **any food** left in the house.

2.4. Pronouns

> **Definition of a pronoun**:
>
> A **pronoun** is a little word that stands **in place of** a noun, a phrase or even a clause, in order to avoid repetition. It agrees in number and gender with the noun, phrase or clause that it replaces, which is called the *antecedent*. The pronoun refers to its logical antecedent in a sentence or paragraph, or in the context of dialogue. Within a sentence, the logical antecedent is most often the preceding or most recent noun. Occasionally the "antecedent" can come after the pronoun referring to it.

2.4.1. Personal pronouns

Personal pronouns in English are fairly easy to master. However it is important to remember that for the third person singular, the choice of pronoun depends on the **gender of the antecedent**: *he* (etc.) if it refers to a man or male or unknown person, *she* if it refers to a female, and *it* for everything else.

The feminine pronouns *she / her / hers* are only used with **humans** (*a lady,* etc.), or with a few animated or moving creatures or objects to which the English language can give a quality of femininity (examples *dog, cat, boat*).   The object pronoun is also used after prepositions.

♣ Do not confuse **possessive pronouns** (used **in place of** a noun) **with possessive adjectives** - in the final column - (which **precede** a noun).

	Subject pronoun	Object pronoun	Possessive pronoun	Possessive adjective
1st person sg.	I	me	mine	my
2nd person sg.	you	you	yours	your
3rd person sg.	he, she, it, one	him, her, it, one*	his, hers, its, –	his, her, its, one's
1st person pl.	we	us	ours	our
2nd person pl.	you	you	yours	your
3rd person pl.	they	them	theirs	their

Examples: Pronouns are in bold, their antecedents are underlined. Possessive adjectives are in blue.

Look at that <u>man</u>. Can you see **him**? **He**'s over there, and that's his wife
with **him**.

There are two bikes in <u>Peter's</u> garage; the green bike is **his** and the blue
one is **mine**.

<u>We</u> 've lost our way; can you help **us** please?

Have **you** seen my <u>phone</u>? I can't see **mine**, but **yours** is over there.

One should always bring a map with **one**, in case **one** loses one's way.

<u>I</u> like our new <u>house</u> but I don't like **theirs**; and I didn't like their old one
either

2.4.1.1. The specific case of *one*

The word *one* causes problems not just for students, but for linguists too.
Unlike other pronouns, *one* can be used *like a noun*, to replace a previously
mentioned noun. In the last example given above, we find the phrase,

  *... and I didn't like **their old one** either*

one is not being used as a pronoun, since it is preceded by a determiner
(*their*) and an adjective (*old*). It is not a noun either, as it has no intrinsic
meaning outside of its context. Swan, in *Practical English Usage* defines
one as a "substitute word"; others call it a "pro-form". But whatever term we
use to describe it, *one* is a special case.

  In examples of this type, *one* behaves exactly like a noun, and can be
assimilated to a count noun with regard to its usage in the sentence.

2.4.1.2 Reflexive and emphatic pronouns

English has a set of **reflexive pronouns** on the model *myself, yourself,
himself,* etc. These are required when a **direct, indirect, or prepositional
pronoun complement** of a verb refers back to the subject, as in:

He convinced **himself** that the exam would be too difficult.
Since I work for **myself**, I can give **myself** a pay rise.
We're going to treat **ourselves** to a special vacation after Covid.
Have you hurt **yourself** badly ?

Reflexive pronouns can also be used as emphatic pronouns, longer forms
of personal pronouns that can be used for emphasis either **in place of**, or
else **in addition to,** a personal pronoun or noun.

I myself do not actually agree with his version of the story.
Do it **yourself**
I could not find **the book** itself**,** so I bought a similar title.

Occasionally an emphatic pronoun is used to emphasize a pronoun that is linked with a noun.

> Peter **and myself** work together as a team.
> Do you mean that it was given **to your father** **and yourself**?

But this is not always considered as good style; a normal pronoun, as in *Peter and I,* will often be considered more acceptable.

Note that while English has **reflexive pronouns**, it does not use reflexive **verbs**. For example there is no English reflexive equivalent of Spanish *lavarse* or French *se laver,* (= *wash*, not *wash oneself),* nor of German *sich freuen* (= *be happy*) except when used for special emphasis.

2.4.1.3. Indefinite pronouns

There are other pronouns similar to personal pronouns, and generally used like personal pronouns; these are indefinite pronouns or impersonal pronouns: they include words such as *someone, anyone, anything, whoever,* (see also § 2.6.1.3.), and even **numbers** or **quantifiers used as pronouns**, such as *many, enough* or *plenty or all*.

Examples

> **Someone** told me you're going to New York next week.
> I can't see **anything.**
> **Whoever** said that was obviously not telling the truth.
> I ordered six boxes, but I've only received **three**.
> **Plenty** was said at the meeting, but the directors couldn't agree.
> He can say complete nonsense, but **many** will still believe him.
> His ideas are complete nonsense, and **few** believe him.
> **Enough** is **enough.**
> **All** is not lost…… **All** you need is Love.

2.4.1.4. Gender neutral pronouns

Sometimes we need to use a third-person singular pronoun to refer to a person, without knowing if the person is male or female, or without wanting to specify the gender. For obvious reasons, we can't use **he** or **she**; but we can't use **it** either, as it is not a gender-neutral personal pronoun, but refers to an object. The classic solution in English is to use **they / them / their** as a singular pronoun: note however that while these pronouns can take on a singular meaning, they are still used in the normal way, as if they referred to a plural entity.

Avoid using the sometimes-used "his or her": this is not considered to be good style, even if it is just occasionally necessary.

Examples

If someone phones, tell **them** to call back later.

If anyone tries to open the safe, **they**'ll get a big surprise.

Each member of the committee gave **their** opinion.

2.4.1.5. The expletive pronoun *there*

There is known as an **expletive** **pronoun** or *dummy* pronoun; this means that it does not refer to a noun or antecedent that has already been mentioned; it refers to a noun object or complement that **has not yet been specified**. It is a third person pronoun, but can be either used as a singular or as a plural, depending on the noun to which it refers. **There** is normally only used with the verb **be**, it can be used with any tense of the verb **be**, including **be** preceded by a modal verb. Just occasionally it can be used with certain other verbs, such as **go, live, stand** or **appear**.

Examples

There was an enormous explosion.

There are thirteen mistakes in your spelling test.

I think that there is a hole in my bucket.

I think that there are some people coming.

There was a strong smell of smoke in the room.

There will be no prizes for students who fail the exam.

There can be no doubt that many top golfers get paid too much.

There must be a faster way than that.

Is there any point in filling in all these long forms?

In the town where I was born (there) lived a man….

Look! There goes Peter.

There appear to be three different types of fish in this pond.

Beside the house there stood a very old oak tree.

2.4.1.6. Interrogative pronouns.

See <u>§ 4.2.1.</u> **Word order in questions**.

2.4.2. Relative pronouns & adjectives

Who, which, that, whoever, what *and others*

See also § 4.6. **Relative clauses** and § 4.2.1. **Interrogative pronouns and determiners.**

2.4.2.1. Relative pronouns - Functions and forms

In their most common usage, relative pronouns introduce a relative clause - either as a subject *(who, which, that)* , or as a direct object *(whom, which, that)*, or in the context of a prepositional phrase *(to whom, with which, by which,* etc.). They are called "**relative**" because in a declarative sentence, they **relate** to a noun that has normally just been mentioned.

The most common and most recognised relative pronouns are who, whom, whose, which and that.

Relating to ▶	Animate (person).	Inanimate (thing).	Either
Subject pronouns	who	which	that
Object pronouns	Whom (who[1])	which	that (or omission)
Pronouns after prepositions	(to, with, by...) whom	(to, with, by...) which	
Possessive relative pronouns	*These do not exist*		
Possessive relative adjectives	whose	of which	whose

Note 1. **The case of** whom: in many varieties of spoken English the **object pronoun** whom is disappearing, replaced by that, or omitted. The word whom survives nonetheless in standard written English, and after prepositions.

Whom has disappeared most notably from direct questions. Few native English speakers would ask *Whom did you see yesterday?* Most would ask: *Who did you see yesterday?*

Examples

This is the man *who* sold me a stolen cellphone.
There were several people at the party, *whom* I'd never met before.

There were a lot of people (*that*) I'd never met before
The machine, *which* had been running non-stop for 3 days, just stopped.
The machine, *that* had been running for 3 days, just stopped.
I know the man *to whom* you were talking.
I was in a complex situation, *from which* I could see no way out.
The events *that* occurred on Friday were rather alarming.

Take care!   The word **whose** is never found on its own at the start of a relative clause: however it can be used as a **possessive relative adjective**, qualifying a noun.

Examples

The President, *whose* **wife** was a movie star, was not very popular.
He found a very old statue *whose* **age** was impossible to determine.
We cannot say:
~~This is my elder brother, whose I was talking~~
We have to use the prepositional form with *of* (or another preposition):
This is my elder brother *of whom* I was talking.

2.4.2.2.   Nominal relative pronouns *What whatever etc.*

1. *What*

What is used as a "**nominal relative pronoun**" (also called "free relative pronoun"). It is a single word which combines the <u>antecedent</u> (stated or implied) *and* the <u>relative pronoun</u>. Thus it corresponds for instance, to French *ce que* or Spanish *lo que, el que* etc.

Examples

After *what* happened yesterday, you ought to be more careful.
You'll have to manage with *what* you can find.
What he said was rather interesting.

2. *Whoever, whatever, whichever*

Though they are less common than *what*, **whoever whatever** and **whichever** are all used as nominal personal pronouns, standing in the place of a noun + relative clause.

Examples

> **Whoever** heard such an ridiculous argument?
>   *Meaning*: Is there any person who heard such a ridiculous argument?
> **Whoever** lost the key ought to find it again pretty quickly.
>   *Meaning*: The person who lost the key ought.....
> **Whatever** you say, I'm not going to change my opinion.
>   *Meaning*: You can say anything that you want, but I'm....
> We'll give the prize to **whoever** gets the right answer first.
> You'll have to manage with **whatever** you can find.
> He'll take **whichever** he prefers.

2.4.2.3. Relative adjectives

1. *Whose, what and which*

Whose is the possessive relative adjective, as noted above. **What** and **which** can also be used as relative adjectives, at the start of a relative clause.

Examples

> Do you know *what* languages he speaks?
> I don't know *which* train to take.
> The President knows *which* people he wants to talk to.
> Nobody could understand **to** *which* laws he was referring.
>   *(or ..... understand which laws he was referring **to**.)*
> He reached the village, **at** *which* point he stopped for a drink.

2. *Whichever and whatever*

Whichever and **whatever** - but **NOT** *whoever* - can also be used as relative adjectives, standing before a noun.

Examples

> **Whichever** team wins, he'll be a happy man.!
>   *Meaning*: The team **that** wins can be one or the other, and
>   he'll still be a happy man.
> We'll have to stay in **whatever** hotel we can find.
>   *Meaning*: We'll have to stay in any hotel **which** we can find
> My Dad's promised to buy me **whatever** laptop I want if I pass my exam.

2.4.2.4. *When, why, where* **and** *how*

Many students are surprised to learn that **when, why, where** and **how**, and also the longer forms **whenever, wherever** and **however**, also function as nominal relative pronouns. As relative pronouns, they are used to replace a longer phrase that would include a standard relative pronoun such as **whom** or **which**.

Examples

We don't know **when** he's coming.
    Meaning: We don't know the time **at which** he's coming.
Can you explain **why** you did that?
    Meaning: Can you explain **for what** reason you did that?
I can't remember **where** I left my car.
    Meaning: I can't remember the place **in which** I left my car.
In the town **where** I was born, lived a man[1] who sailed to sea.
    From the Beatles' song Yellow Submarine.
I hope you know **how** to mend it!
    Meaning: I hope you know the way **in which** to mend it?
Whenever his son comes to stay, they go out to a good restaurant.
    Meaning: **Each time that** his son comes....
Wherever he goes, he leaves a trail of damage behind him.
    Meaning: In **every place to which h**e goes, he leaves .....
However I try, I can't get the right answer.
    Meaning: In spite of all the ways in **which** I have tried, I can't get...

2.4.3. Relative adverb: **however**

However can also be used as a relative adverb, qualifying an adjective or adverb.

However hard I try, I can't manage to find the right answer!
    Meaning: I can't find the answer even if I try in ways which are very hard. We'll have plenty of food **however** many people actually come.
    Meaning: The number of people who come is not important, we'll have...

---

1. *Lived a man…* Why is the subject after the verb? Because this is poetry, where word order is not always respected. Also, because *lived* means *there lived,* so the real subject is not *a man*, but the expletive pronoun *there* (see § 2.4.1.4 above)

2.4.4. Demonstrative pronouns and adjectives

2.4.4.1. Demonstrative pronouns

1. There are four demonstrative pronouns in English, two in the singular, and two in the plural; they indicate either proximity (*this, these*), or distance (*that, those*).

	Proximity	Distance
Singular	This	That
Plural	These	Those

It is important to understand what is meant by **proximity and distance**. The notion of proximity can be <u>grammatical</u> (referring to something close in the sentence), <u>spatial</u> (something close to the speaker) or <u>temporal</u> (close in time).

Examples

> *This* is her car, and **that** (*further away*) is mine.
> I don't like *these* (*in front of me*) but I do like *those* (*further away*).
> Our car has broken down, and it's snowing. *This* (*the situation in which we find ourselves*) is not a good situation.
> He wrote about many places, including some small Greek islands; *these* (*direct antecedent in the sentence*), he said, were his favourite places.
> *That* (*= what you have just said*) is not a very intelligent idea.

2. Demonstrative pronouns <u>cannot</u> be preceded by adjectives nor by possessives, but **that** and **those** can be followed by prepositional phrases starting with **of** or **in** or other prepositions. See possessive structures below.
   We cannot say *Peter's those*, nor *His that* nor *blue these*; we have to say *Those of Peter*, or *that one of his*, or *these blue ones*.

2.4.4.2. Possessive structures: the demonstrative pronoun followed by "of"

> ▶ First note this important rule:
>   This and these are never followed by of:
>   For example, we can not say:
>   ~~My apple is ripe, this of my sister is not.~~

In possessive structures, usage depends whether we are dealing with attribution or possession.

With attribution

The only normal structure with demonstrative pronouns is to use that of or those of:

> His reputation was bigger than that of Elvis.
> While Japan's development was rapid, that of Singapore was even faster.
> The title of his first book was "Blue Waves", that of the second was "Deep
>   Oceans".

With possession

The most common structure, particularly in spoken English, is to use .....'s or (…'s one(s)).

> My books are new, John's (ones) are old.
>   Not: ~~My books are new, those of John are old~~
> Our shirts are white: the other team's ones are red.

That of / those of tend to be only used in formal contexts (▶ see § 4.8. Style) , particularly written English:

> The first tourist's papers were in order, but those of the remaining
>   tourists were not.

2.4.4.3.   Demonstrative pronoun phrases

Demonstrative pronouns (most commonly those) can be the headwords of phrases in which they are followed by various prepositions or by a relative clause.

In Demonstrative pronoun phrases, the singular demonstrative pronouns that and this must normally be reinforced by the addition of one to become **this one** or **that one**. This is also possible for **these ones** or **those ones** (but the *one* is not essential).

> Look at those paintings: I prefer **those / those** (ones) on the left.
> This book is mine, but **that one** **on the table** is yours.
> *We cannot say:* ~~This book is mine, but that on the table is yours.~~
> All **those in** **favor**, raise your hand.
> I like **these** (ones) **with** **the strong peppermint flavor**.
> Take as many as you want; **those that** **are still here tonight** will be
>   destroyed.
> **Those who** **have finished their project** can go home.
> All **those who** **want to help** should be here tomorrow morning at nine.
> Look at **these** (ones) **that** **I made yesterday**.

2.4.4.4. Demonstrative adjectives

► **This (these)** and **that (those)** can also be used as demonstrative adjectives: the same principles of proximity and distance apply.

Examples

> **This** book is mine, **that** book is yours.
> **These** students come from Paraguay.
> I really like **those** new trains they're using now.

"**One**" is sometimes used as a pro-form, to avoid repeating a noun.

> **This** book is mine, **that one** is yours

or even (if the context makes it quite clear what is being referred to)

> **This one** is mine, **that one** Is yours.

The definite article **the**, rather than a demonstrative adjective, can also be used with a demonstrative value

> **This one** is mine, yours is **the one** on the table.

2.5. Articles

Articles belong to the larger category of words known as **determiners**. Unlike other common types of determiner (*numbers, demonstratives, quantifiers*), articles cannot stand alone. They must be followed by a noun.

2.5.1. Article usage

The basic rules:
Basically, the rules for using articles in English are quite simple:
1. If a noun is used in a "**specified**" or restricted context, **a determiner is required** – most commonly the **definite** article.
2. When a noun is used in an "**unspecified**" or generalizing context, in some cases an **indefinite article** is required, in others no article at all.

2.5.2. The definite article

 How simple English is! There is only <u>one</u> definite article, and that is "**the**"; the only difficulty is knowing when to use it, and when it is not needed (see § 2.5.4 below.)

2.5.3. The indefinite article

English has **two** indefinite articles**, a** and **an.**
   a is used before nouns starting with a consonant or a semivowel,
   an is used before nouns starting with a phonetic vowel.

Examples: *a dog, a cat, an apple, an orange, an uncle*, but **a** university (because the word *university* starts with phonetic [ju:], which is not a vowel). Indefinite articles can only be used with **count nouns**. They are used when a count noun in the singular refers to a **non-specified or non defined entity.**

Examples

   a) There's *a plane* (= unspecified) due in 5 minutes. It's *the* plane (= specified) from Denver.
   b) Look! I can see *a hotel* over there! (= an unspecified hotel) It's *the* hotel (= specified) we're looking for!.

There is **no indefinite article in the plural**. The word "some" is occasionally referred to as a plural indefinite article, but really it is a quantifier **(like many, few, etc.).**

2.5.4. Is an article even necessary ?

Before deciding which article to use, it is first necessary to determine if it is indeed necessary to use any article at all. This will depend on what type of noun is being used, a **count** noun or a **non-count** noun (see § 2.3. above), and if it is a count noun, whether it is a generalization or not.

1. Count nouns are nouns referring to items that can be counted, for example: *One car, two pens, three people, four guitars, five hotels etc.* These nouns can be used in the singular or the plural.

- **In the singular,** count nouns **must** be preceded by a determiner:

> **The** dog is happy   *or*   **This** dog is happy, etc.
>   *but not:* ~~Dog is happy.~~
> I'm reading **my** book   *or*   I'm reading **the** book ;
>   *but not:* ~~I'm reading book~~

- **In the plural,** they **may** **require a determiner,** depending on context (whether or not they are generalizations).

2. Non-count nouns are nouns referring to abstractions, substances or generalizations, for example: *Oxygen, health, money, heat, astronomy.*

- **In the singular,** non-count nouns do not require a determiner.

- The plural is even easier: non-count nouns can NOT usually be used in the plural.

2.5.5. Articles and quantifiers

Although articles are determiners, and the general rule is "*A noun is only preceded by one determiner*", there are cases where the definite article can be preceded by a **secondary determiner** in the form of a **quantifier** or a **number.**

Examples

> a) Some of the tomatoes are red.
> b) Both of the children are very tired.
> c) Three of the machines were out of order.

2.6. Quantifiers

> **Definition**
>
> Quantifiers are a type of determiner which denote imprecise quantity.
> They modify nouns or pronouns. They differ from **numbers** or numerals
> which indicate precise quantity.
> Before pronouns, quantifiers are always followed by of.

The most common quantifiers used in English are:
some / any , much, many, a lot, a few, several, enough.

2.6.1. Some and any, their compounds and other neutral quantifiers

In many cases, some is used as a plural indefinite article, the plural of "a" or "an"; but more often, some implies a limited quantity, and for this reason has the value of a neutral quantifier, neither big nor small nor specific.

Some is used in affirmative statements;
it is replaced with any in negative and interrogative contexts. **Examples:**

> I've got some apples in my basket and some water in my bottle.
> I haven't got any apples in my basket, nor any water in my bottle.
> Have you got any apples in your basket? Have you got any water in your bottle?
> We had some visitors last month, but we didn't have any this month.
> Have you got any rooms free for the night of May 30th?

2.6.1.1. Special cases

Some and any used in the subject of an affirmative statement....

- As a singular subject, some implies a non-determined or non-specified entity (examples 1 - 4 below) , any implies a singular but potentially plural entity (see examples 5 - 8 below).

- Used with count nouns in the plural, some just has the function of a plural indefinite article (example 9). Any used with a plural subject has the meaning of *all.... if there are any* (example 10).

Examples

<table>
<tr><td>

Some child has left his coat on the bus.
Some help would be appreciated. (= Will someone please help me.)
Some famous politician once said, "To vote or not to vote?"
Even with the best insulation, **some** heat always escapes.
Any help would be appreciated.
    (= If someone actually helped me, that would be good)
Any accident at high speed can be fatal.
Almost **any** child will say yes if you offer an ice-cream
Any educated person knows who Shakespeare was.
Some people are intelligent.
Any volunteers should sign up by Friday at the latest.

</td></tr>
</table>

2.6.1.2. *Any* or *no*

- In a **negative statement** in English, negation is normally expressed through the verb; negation can however be expressed by adding a negative value to the subject or the direct object of the sentence.
- Whenever negation is expressed in a noun phrase, the verbal negative particle *not* is replaced by the negative quantifier **no**. ▶ For more on this see § 4.5.3. Negation using nouns.

Examples

<table>
<tr><td>

There **aren't any** children in the road.
    = There **are** *no* **children** in the road.
You **mustn't** bring **any** maps with you on the expedition.
    = You **must** bring **no** maps with you on the expedition.
I'm **not going** to visit **any** castles in Scotland.
    = I'm **going** to visit **no** castles in Scotland.
Cellphones **are not allowed** in the exam room.
    = *No* cellphones **are allowed** in the exam room.

</td></tr>
</table>

2.6.1.3. Compound forms of some, any and no

Some any and **no** can be compounded with other words to form **indefinite pronoun**s (see § 2.4.1.3.) ; these **pronouns** can be <u>followed</u> by a **qualifying adjective.** The most common compounds are

- Someone, anyone, no one
- Something, anything, nothing

Exactly the same principles apply to these compounds, as apply to **some, any** or **no** used on their own.

Examples:

Affirmation:

> There **is something** in the cupboard.
> I **put** my phone down **somewhere**.
> I've got **something important** to tell you

Negation:

> There **isn't anything** in the cupboard.
> There**'s nothing** in the cupboard.

Interrogation:

> **Is** there **anything** in the cupboard?
> **Can** you **see** my telephone **anywhere**?
> Well, can you tell us **anything new**?

2.6.1.4. *Some in an interrogative sentence*

In certain interrogative sentences (questions), **some** may be able to replace **any**.

When **some (...)** is used instead of **any (...)**, the speaker is predicting that the coming answer will be <u>affirmative</u>; if the same question were asked using **any**, the speaker would not be predicting any specific reply.

Examples

Is there **someone** in the room?
> *(= I think there is someone here; am I right?)*
Is there **anyone** in the room?
> *(= I don't know if anyone is here; can someone tell me?)*
Would you like **some** tea?   (An affirmative answer is expected) .

2.6.1.5. With *of: Some of, any of, none of*

When **some, any** or **none** (but never **no**) are followed by the word **of**, the following noun must be introduced by an article or other determiner; a following **pronoun** will not of course need a determiner.

Examples

Some of *the* children are eating sweets.
    = **Some** children are eating sweets.
Are any of *the* children eating sweets?
    = Are **any** children eating sweets?
None of *the* actors like working in this theatre.
    = **No** actors like working in this theatre.
I can answer some of *the* questions; he can't answer any of them.

Other determiners can also follow some of / any of / none of:

Some of John's cars are very old.
Some of my cars are very old.
Some of these cars are very old.

Note that some of and none of are **never** normally followed **directly** by a noun.

- **One cannot say**: ~~Some of children~~... ~~None of animals~~... etc.

2.6.1.6. *Other neutral quantifiers:*

Several, a number of, enough   These quantifiers are dealt with under the section quantifiers of large quantity. Most commonly they express a *large or sufficiently large quantity*, often they are used with a very neutral meaning, as synonyms of some or any.

2.6.2. Large quantity quantifiers

 much, many, lots of, plenty of, numerous, a large number of, etc.

2.6.2.1 *Much and many (without of):*

Much is used with non-count nouns (always in the singular); many is used with count nouns in the plural. (See ▶ § 2.3. the difference between count nouns and non-count nouns).

Much and many in affirmative statements

In modern spoken English, much, and to a lesser extent many are not often used as quantifiers before nouns in <u>affirmative</u> statements, unless introduced by an intensifier, notably so or too , or followed by of;

Examples

> I have **many** reasons for thinking that this man is innocent
>> *This is acceptable, but rather formal; most English speakers would more naturally say:*
>
> **I have plenty of / a lot of / ample /** reasons for thinking .....
>
> **Much** whisky is of very good quality.
>> *This sentence is technically acceptable, but not probable in modern spoken English. Most people would say (and write):*
>
> **A lot** of whisky / **A good proportion** of whisky / **Plenty** of whisky.
>
> He has **much** money.
>> *This is **not** normal English. Speakers would more naturally say:*
>
> He has **a lot of** money / He has **loads of** money.... etc.
>
> There is **so much** poverty in the world.
> There are **too many** people in here.
>> *These examples, with **so** and **too**, are perfectly normal English.*

Remember: don't use **much** or **many** in affirmative statements, if you can avoid it. Though their use may be possible, it often sounds very formal, old-fashioned or strange in modern English.

Much and many in negative statements and questions

Much, and **many** are more commonly used in interrogative and negative contexts, and most particularly in the interrogative expressions **how much** and **how many**.

Examples

> We **don't have much** time to finish this.
> There are **not many** people who know the answer to this.
> **Did you have much** luck ?
> **How much does** this tee-shirt cost?
> **How many times do** I have to tell you not to do that ?

2.6.2.2. *Much of / many of* When is *"of"* needed ?

IMPORTANT ! If they **come before a second determiner** such as an article, a possessive or a demonstrative, or before a **pronoun**, **much** and **many** **must** be followed by **of**. The same principle applies to *few / few of* (see below), *some / some of,* etc.

Examples

> I can't see **many** people.
> I can't see **many of my** friends
> **Many** houses were destroyed in the war.
>   *but* **Many of the** houses were destroyed in the war.
> They didn't drink **much** beer
>   *but* They didn't drink **much of that** beer we gave them.
> **As many of you** already know, last night ….
> **Much** of **what** you have written is very good.
>   *This is quite acceptable in a formal context, but in spoken and less*
>   *formal written style, most English-speakers would say (and write)*
>   *something like:*
> **A lot of** what you have written……
> **A good deal of** what you have written…..

Much of and **many of cannot** be used <u>directly before</u> nouns.

Examples: **one cannot say:**

> ~~Much of whiskey~~ is very expensive
> ~~Many of people~~ are waiting for you.

2.6.2.3. *Lots of, a lot of, plenty of, a large number of, numerous*

These expressions are all more or less synonyms. In the paragraph title above, they are arranged in order of formality, going from the most informal (**lots of**) to the most formal (**numerous**). Informal language is more appropriate in dialogue, formal language in written documents.

2.6.2.4. *Several **and** a number of*

These imply "*more than one, but less than a lot*". They are not usually used in negative or interrogative structures, only in affirmative statements.

Examples

> There are **several** books / **a number of** books by J.K.Rowling in our
>   library.
> **Several** people / **A number of** people said that they'd seen the missing
>   child.
> **Several of us** wanted to stop because the weather was so bad.

2.6.3. Small quantity quantifiers

Few, a few, little, a little, not many, not much, etc.

Except for **not much** or **not many**, these quantifiers are generally used in **affirmative statements.**

- **Little, a little, not much** are used with non-count nouns (always in the singular).
- **Few, a few, not many** are used with count nouns or pronouns in the plural.
- **Few** and **little** imply a quantity which is essentially small or *smaller than expected*.
- **A few** and **a little** imply small quantity, but *possibly more than expected*.

Examples

> **Few** people can speak more than three languages.
> **A few** (of the) paintings in this gallery are really good.
> There's **little** point in trying to mend it. You'll never succeed!
> I've got **a little** money left; let's go and have a drink.
> There's not **much** point in waiting for him to come.

2.6.3.1. *Few or a few, little or a little?*

The difference between the two expressions in each phrase is purely one of **meaning**, not of **usage**.

Without the article, *few* and *little* (used respectively with count nouns and non-count nouns) have the meaning of "*not much/ not many, and possibly less than one might hope for or expect*". These expressions have a negative value to them.

With the article, *a few* and *a little* have the meaning of "*at least some, perhaps more than one might expect*". These expressions have a positive value.

Examples

> **Few** of my friends were there, so I was disappointed.
> **A few** of my friends were there, so I was quite happy.
> **A few** of them were there, so I was quite happy.
> Hurry up; there's **little** time left!
> We have **a little** time to spare, so let's stop and have a cup of coffee.

2.6.4. Neutral and relative quantifiers

Neutral quantifiers do not indicate either a large quantity or a small quantity: they are not really concerned by actual quantity, only by **relative** quantity. They are dealt with in four different groups:

    Some and any (see § 2.6.1 above)
    Each and every
    All and whole
    Most, most of and **enough**

2.6.4.1. *Each* and *every*

Each and **every** have very similar meanings, but there are important differences of meaning and usage.

Meanings and use of each and every

- **Each** refers to a plural number of people or items, but it considers each person or item as an individual or dissimilar unit, it does not consider the group collectively. **Each can also be used as a pronoun**.
- **Every** also refers to a multiple number of people or items; but it considers these people or items as part of a similar collective group. If there are just two items or people, every may be replaced by both. **Every cannot be used as a pronoun**.

Here are some pairs of sentences that clearly illustrate the difference between each and every. In the first sentence of each pair, the speaker is implying dissimilar or individual actions: in the second of each pair, the speaker is expressing similarity of action or situation.

Examples

> **Each** child was reading a different book. *(dissimilar books)*
> **Every** child was reading a book. *(similar action)*
> You have to fill in details on **each** page individually. *(dissimilar pages)*
> You have to fill in details on **every** page. *(similar action)*
> We go on vacation in a different place **each** summer. *(dissimilar destinations)*
> We go on vacation to Rhode Island **every** summer. *(similar action)*
> He makes a different mistake **each** time. *(dissimilar action)*
> He makes the same mistake **every** time. *(similar action)*

Sometimes it is important to distinguish between *each* and *every*; in other cases, this distinction is not important, and the user can choose either word.

Usage

Both *each* and *every* are **singular** quantifiers. When they determine the subject of a sentence, they normally (but not always) require a verb in the singular.

Examples

> Each member of the committee **was** allowed to speak once.
> Each of us was allowed to speak for five minutes
> Every cloud **has** a silver lining.
> Each day **is** different.
> Every person I know **has** seen the movie.

Particular uses of *each*

Each as a quantifier can be used with three different structures.

- Structure 1 : each + singular noun
- Structure 2 : each + of + plural noun / pronoun
- Structure 3 : Plural noun / pronoun + each

TAKE CARE ! **Singular or plural ?**

When *each* is used in the *subject* of a sentence:

- The verb is in the **singular** if **each** comes before the noun or pronoun (**structures 1** and **2**).

- The verb is in the **plural** if each follows the noun or pronoun that it determines **(structure 3).** When **each** follows a noun or pronoun, it may do so directly, or else be placed between the auxiliary and the verb

Examples

> Structure 1. **Each** child **was** reading a book.
> Structure 2. **Each of the** children **was** reading a book.
>   **Each of us has** a different answer.
> **Structure 3.** The children **were** each reading a book.
>   *or* The children each **were** reading a book.
>   We each **have** provided a different answer.
>   We **have** each provided a different answer.

2.6.4.2. *All and whole*

All and **whole** express totality or completeness.

Sometimes one can choose either of them; but there are major differences in their usage, and *all* and *whole* are not always interchangeable.

- **All** can refer to singular nouns or pronouns, or to plural nouns or pronouns.

- **Whole** is essentially used with nouns in the singular. It is occasionally used as a descriptive adjective with nouns in the plural, and cannot normally be used with pronouns.

1. *All* with *singular nouns.*

There are three structures possible, as in these examples :

- **All day / all the time / all of the day**

Usually a determiner is required, but **of** is not required, and its use depends on context or choice. If **all of** is used with a singular noun, it <u>must</u> be followed by a determiner, as in **all of** <u>the</u> **day,** not ~~all of day.~~

Determiners that can be used in this structure are **the**, demonstrative adjectives (**this, that**), possessive adjectives (**my, your,** etc.), possessive forms of the noun (**Peter's, the man's,** etc.).

When the phrase with **all** is the **subject** of a statement, the verb is normally in the singular – unless the noun in the group is a collective noun referring to multiple people, such as team, committee, school, or family, when the verb is normally in the plural (examples 3,4 and 5).

Examples

1. **All** the factory was on fire.
2. **All** (of) my collection of old books has been stolen.
3. **All** the school know that the principal has won the lottery.
   or **All** the school knows that the principal has won the lottery.
4. **All** my family are coming to dinner tomorrow.
   All my family is coming to dinner tomorrow . sounds improbable
5. **All** the President's team are standing for re-election.
6. **All** (of) this rubbish must be cleared up at once!
7. I want you to clear up **all** (of) this rubbish.
8. **Not all** art is valuable. *Take care! This means* "Some art is not
   valuable": *it does not mean "* **No** works of art are valuable".

2. *All* with *plural nouns*

Plural nouns are by definition count nouns, so the situation is less complicated. There are three structures, as in these examples

- *All children / all the children / all of the children :*

   Whether to use a determiner or not depends on the context, and follows exactly the normal rules for count nouns in the plural. It depends if the noun is being used as an **open** **generalization** (no determiner), examples 1 - 5, or as a **limited** **generalization** (with determiner), examples 6 - 8.

Examples

1. **All** diamonds are valuable
2. **All** fish live in water.
3. I like **all** kinds of music.
4. He gave **all** sorts of excuses for being late.
5. **All** multinational companies have operations in several countries.
6. **All (of) the** diamonds in this shop are very valuable.
7. **All (of) the** fish that I've eaten have been very tasty .
8. I like **all (of) the** music that you play on your violin.

3. *Whole*

Whole as a **quantifier** can only be used with **singular** nouns, either singular count nouns or singular non-count nouns. It is used exactly like a normal adjective, on the models:

- { the + **whole** (+of + determiner) + noun}.
- { the + **whole** (+of + determiner) + adjective +noun}.

Whole has a similar meaning to *all,* though the structures are different.

However, by using *the whole* one stresses the **unity** of an entity, not its multiple components. Thus when the subject of a sentence is a collective noun implying multiple people , such as *team, committee, school,* or *family*, qualified by **whole**, the verb is most often in the singular (contrast this with *all*, above).

Examples with whole

You will tell the truth, the **whole** truth, and nothing but the truth.

This **whole** (of the) story has been made up.

We'll have to repaint the **whole** (of the) room.

There was a **whole** complicated dossier to fill in.

The **whole** (of the) English team was welcomed by the Queen.

4. *Note: Whole and place names:*

The structure {the + **whole** + noun} is **not** used with place names that do not **already** contain an article, notably the names of countries. One can say *the whole United States,* but one **cannot** say *the whole England*: one can say *the **whole of** England.*

Examples:

> `OK` The virus caused thousands of deaths throughout **the whole of the** United States.
> `OK` The virus caused thousands of deaths throughout **the whole** United States.
> `OK` **The whole of** Chicago was put on alert.
> **Not** OK ~~The whole Chicago~~ was put on alert.

2.6.4.3. *Most, most of* **and** *enough*

There are a couple of common quantifiers that express relative or proportional quantity.

Most / most of

These imply *more than half of, a majority of*, or *almost all*. They **do not** mean the same as *many / many of* .

Enough

Enough implies a *sufficient quantity*; it is used in affirmations, negations and questions.

> I've done **enough** work for one day.
> There were **enough** strong men to move the fallen tree.
> We can get tickets for the concert, I've got **enough** money now.
> Have you got **enough** money for the tickets?
> No, I haven't got **enough**.

`TAKE CARE !` *Do not confuse....*

enough as a quantifier adjective <u>preceding</u> a noun, as in

> *I've done enough work for one day.*

with *enough* as an intensifier <u>following</u> an adjective, as in:

> *That's good enough for me.*

2.6.5. Take care: Quantifiers with of...

Much of, many of, few of, a little of, plenty of, lots of, some of, a number of, none of, enough of, several of, etc.

Of is **always** required between a **quantifier** and a **pronoun**, as in:

> **Most of us** were very worried about the pandemic.
>
> As for the spectators, **lots of them** just wanted to go home.

Before **nouns**, there is a choice of two possible structures: With most determiners the choice is between

- *either* {quantifier + noun}
- *or* {quantifier + of + determiner + noun}

BUT With a few quantifiers, such **as a lot, a few, plenty, of** is **always** required, whether there is a determiner or not.

The rule....	... applies to
Either quantifier + noun, **or** quantifier + of + determiner + noun	all, each, some, many, much, (a) few, (a) little, none , several, enough,
Of is **always required**, with or without a determiner	plenty of, a lot of, lots of, a number of, a couple of,

Here are a few examples; most are right, some are **wrong**.

> `OK` **Some of the people** are right **some of the** time, but **all of the people** cannot be right **all of the time**.
>
> **Not OK** ~~Some of people~~ are right ~~some of time~~, ~~but all of people~~ cannot be right ~~all of time~~.
>
> `OK` **Plenty of supporters** came to the match.
>
> `OK` **Plenty of the supporters** came to the match.
>
> **Not OK** ~~Plenty supporters~~ came to the match.
>
> `OK` **Several of the** players were sent off.
>
> `OK` **Several players** were sent off.
>
> **Not OK** ~~Several of players~~ were sent off.
>
> `OK` I'd like **a few of these** apples, please.
>
> `OK` I'd like **a few of your** apples, please.
>
> **Not OK** ~~I'd like **a few of apples**, please.~~
>
> **Not OK** ~~I'd like **few of apples**, please.~~

2.7. Numbers

2.7.1. Cardinal numbers

Cardinal numbers are the numbers that we use for counting or designating quantity: English-speakers use them every day - *one two three four* etc.

Grammatical functions

Cardinal numbers can be used as determiners or **numeral adjectives** in front of nouns, or else as indefinite pronouns. (see § 2.4.1.3.)

Examples

> I ordered **six** boxes, but I've only received **three**.
> **Twenty-five** runners started the race, but only **eleven** finished.

From 0 to 100 - From zero to a hundred

The number **0** is variously expressed as **nought** (in British English) or **zero** (in all forms of English): in the middle of a series of digits, it may also be pronounced "**oh**". Everyone has heard of James Bond, also known as **007**. That is pronounced "**double-oh-seven**" or "**oh-oh-seven**", but never "*nought-nought-seven*" nor "*zero-zero-seven*".

Here are the important cardinal numbers between one and a hundred, which can serve as models for other numbers.

1	one	11	eleven	21	twenty-one
2	two	12	twelve	22	twenty-two
3	three	13	thirteen	30	thirty
4	four	14	fourteen	40	forty
5	five	15	fifteen	50	fifty
6	six	16	sixteen	60	sixty
7	seven	17	seventeen	70	seventy
8	eight	18	eighteen	80	eighty
9	nine	19	nineteen	90	ninety
10	ten	20	twenty	100	a hundred

TAKE CARE ! Watch out for spelling: **fourteen** but **forty**.

Numbers from 101 to 999 - three-digit numbers

> **Important:** the examples and rules below illustrate **American** usage. In the **USA**, the word *and* is normally omitted. A hyphen (-) is normally used in numbers between 21 and 99, whether these stand alone or are part of a larger number. In British English, **and** is added after the word *hundred* or *thousand*

From the following examples, all other three-digit numbers in English can be formed.

101	a hundred (and) one	365	three hundred (and) sixty-five
111	a hundred (and) eleven	480	four hundred (and)eighty
121	a hundred (and) twenty-one	545	five hundred (and) forty-five
133	a hundred (and) thirty-three	644	six hundred (and) forty-four
257	two hundred (and) fifty-seven	799	seven hundred (and) ninety-nine

Notes:

In British English, the word **hundred**, except as a round number (a number ending in **00**), is always followed by "**and**", both in spoken English and in written English when numbers are written out as words.

The word **hundred** never takes an "**s**" as part of a cardinal number.
For numbers between 100 and 199, one normally says "**a hundred**" and not "**one hundred**".
The expression **one hundred** is used only to put emphasis on the figure **one** (i.e. *one*, not two nor three), or to stress the word.

Example:

> I counted **one** hundred (and) twenty planes   (and not 220 nor 320).

Hundreds in the plural

The words **hundred, thousand** and **million** never take an **s** in the plural as cardinal numbers (which are a form of adjective). They only take an **s** when used as nouns designating an **imprecise quantity** of hundreds or thousands, etc., followed by *of* ...

Examples

There are hundred**s of** ducks on the lake.

Thousand**s of** people crammed into the stadium.

These sentences do not say *how many* hundreds nor *how many* thousands: the "**s**" is the only mark of plurality.

Numbers from 1000 to 1,000,000

- Apart from round numbers (numbers ending in 00) numbers above 1000 are normally written in **figures**, not in words. *They are written in words here as a means to show how they are used in spoken English.*

1000	a thousand	4656	four thousand six hundred (and) fifty-six
1001	a thousand and one	10,000	ten thousand
1086	one thousand (and) eighty-six	10,148	ten thousand one hundred (and) forty-eight
1147	one thousand one hundred (and) forty-seven	65,423	sixty-five thousand four hundred (and) twenty-three
1201	one thousand two hundred (and) one	100,000	A hundred thousand
3600	three thousand six hundred	699,482	Six hundred (and) ninety-nine thousand four hundred (and) eighty-two

Reminder: examples and rules including the word "and" reflect usage in British / international English.

In **American English,** the word *and* is usually omitted.

- **After 1000**, if the word "**hundred**" does not occur in the number, it is the word **thousand** which is followed by **and**.

- **Apart from round numbers** (1000, 7000 etc.) there will always be an **and** somewhere in the number in British English, though not in **American English**.

- In British English the word **hundred** is always followed by "and" once it is followed by another digit, and *even if it occurs more than once* in the number. **American English** does not require this *and*.

- Whether writing in figures or in words, with numbers of more than four digits it is normal to put a **comma** every three digits. The comma is optional with four-digit numbers.

Examples;

1018 = One thousand (**and**) eighteen

43,003 = forty-three thousand (**and**) three

56,100 = fifty-six thousand one hundred

25,864 = Twenty-five thousand eight hundred (**and**) sixty-four

654,122 = Six hundred (**and**) fifty-four thousand, one hundred (**and**)
   twenty-two

- In numbers **from 1100 to 1199**, the figure **1** is usually pronounced in full, **one** and not a, before the words **thousand** and **hundred.**
- **Four-digit numbers below 2000** (and rarely above) may sometimes also be expressed starting with "**eleven hundred**", "twelve hundred", etc. This is the normal way of expressing the **year** in dates.

Examples

1618 = One thousand six hundred (and)eighteen, *or*
The year sixteen (hundred and) eighteen

Numbers greater than a million

The same principles apply. The number simply starts with a quantity of millions (or billions) for example *One million...*or *Twenty-five million...* or *Eight hundred twenty million...*or *two billion*

Examples

1,002,018 = One million two thousand (and) eighteen

1,001,116 = One million one thousand one hundred (and) sixteen.

736,654,121 = Seven hundred and thirty-six million, six hundred (and)
    fifty-four thousand, one hundred (and) twenty-one

In British English, the word **hundred** is always followed by "**and**" unless it is round (with "00"), no matter how often it occurs in the number.

2.7.2. Ordinal numbers

Numerical adjectives of order

Ordinals are words like *first, second, third*.....

They are adjectives formed from cardinal numbers. They are used to indicate the position of an entity in a stated or implied series.

In common usage, written as figures, they are formed by a number followed by an abbreviated ending corresponding to the ending of the written word. In most cases the ending is **th**; but this is not always the case . Ordinals derived from cardinals in **–y** (such as **twenty**) end in **–ieth**.

Ordinals are also used to express fractions and dates. In the case of fractions, the endings are not written when the fractions are expressed in figures.

From 1st to 100th

Here are the main ordinals in English, up to **hundredth**; from these examples all others can be formed.

1st	first	11th	eleventh	21st	twenty-first
2nd	second	12th	twelve	22nd	twenty-second
3rd	third	13th	thirteenth	33rd	thirty-third
4th	fourth	14th	fourteenth	44th	forty-fourth
5th	fifth	15th	fifteenth	50th	fiftieth
6th	sixth	16th	sixteenth	60th	sixtieth
7th	seventh	17th	seventeenth	71st	seventy-first
8th	eighth	18th	eighteenth	82nd	eighty-second
9th	ninth	19th	nineteenth	99th	ninety-ninth
10th	tenth	20th	twentieth	100th	a hundredth

Ordinals after 100th

From these examples you can see how all ordinals are formed.

101st	hundred (and) first	365th	three hundred (and) sixty-fifth
111th	hundred (and) eleventh	500th	five hundredth
121st	hundred (and) twenty first	545th	five hundred (and) forty-fifth
133rd	hundred (and) thirty-third	644th	six hundred (and) forty-fourth
257th	two hundred (and) fifty-seventh	999th	nine hundred (and) ninety nine
302nd	three hundred (and) second	1250th	one thousand two hundred (and) fiftieth

Note: ordinals can be preceded by a range of different articles or determiners

Examples

The first anniversary - the 1st anniversary
My twenty-first birthday - My 21st birthday
Three hundredths of a second - 3/100 of a second.
My hundred second attempt - My 102nd attempt.
The US Hundred first Airborne division - The US 101st Airborne division
You are our millionth visitor. You are our 1,000,000th visitor

Other points to note:

Translating numbers into other languages.

The basic rule is simple: translate using <u>words</u> when the original number is written in <u>words</u>, translate using <u>figures</u> when the original uses <u>figures</u>.

Examples

The three musketeers = Les trois mousquetaires.
My 21st birthday - Mein 21. Geburtstag.
Three hundredths of a second - Tres centésimas de segundo
His 203rd attempt - Zijn 203 poging.
The US Hundred first Airborne division - La cent-unième division US
    aeroportée.

2.7.3. Fractions & decimals

1. Fractions

Fractions, **which express quantities less than one**, should not cause many problems for students of English, once they have understood how they are formed.

Except for the most common fractions, ¼ ½ and ¾, fractions are made up of a cardinal number (one, two, three etc.) followed by an ordinal , usually in the plural (thirds, fifths, sixths etc.) Here are the most common fractions in English, and a few others as random examples.

1/4	a quarter (occasionally a fourth)	3/16	three sixteenths
1/2	a half	1/32	one thirty-second
3/4	three quarters	7/9	seven ninths
1/3	a third	1/100	a hundredth or one hundredth
2/3	two thirds	12/100	twelve hundredths
3/8	three eighths	21/1000	twenty-one thousandths

Fractions are used in all styles of language, including scientific and technical English. In particular, North Americans, notably people in the USA, have not fully adopted the decimal system like most of the rest of the world, and still use non-metric measurements such as feet and inches.... and fractions of these.

Examples

Half a pint of beer
A quarter of a second
Three quarters of a mile
Three fifths of the contents of the bottle
A thickness of one thirty-second of an inch
A tolerance of six thousandths of a millimeter

2 Decimals

Decimals are regularly used in everyday English, but more specifically in scientific and technical English, in order to indicate with precision quantities that are not a complete number. They are not difficult to use.

After **the decimal point** figures are normally expressed digit by digit, though sometimes, specially in American English, in pairs The words **hundred** and **thousand** are never used after the decimal point.

Note that the decimal **point** is precisely that; a **point**, not a comma. **Before** a decimal point, for a quantity less than 1, one normally begins (British English) **nought point** ... or (all forms of English) **zero point** .... But **after** the decimal point, the **0** is expressed as "**oh**" or "**zero**" (or "**nought**" in British English).

0.25	point two five *or* zero point two five *or* point twenty-five	8.56	eight point five six *or* eight point fifty-six
0.5	point five, *or* zero point five	12.15	twelve point one five *or* twelve point fifteen
0.75	point seven five, *or* zero point seven five, *or* zero point seventy-five	17.806	seventeen point eight oh six
0.333	point three three three, *or* zero point three three three	384.63	three hundred and eighty-four point six three
0.6405	zero point six four zero five	40.004	Forty point oh oh four *or* Forty point zero zero four
1.5	one point five	117.87659	one hundred and seventeen point eight seven six five nine

Important; except on very rare occasions, figures with decimals are never written out in words, but always written in figures. On this page, examples are expressed in words as a representation of the way they are expressed in spoken English.

Examples

Written; It was 0.2445 mm thick.

Oral; It was (zero) point two four four five millimeters thick.

Written; The long side measures 6.652 in.

Oral; The long side measures six point six five two inches.

Written; The solar vehicle reached a record speed of 131.68 m.p.h.

Oral; The solar vehicle reached a record speed of a hundred (and)thirty-one point six eight miles an hour (or miles per hour).

2.8. Possession

Possessive structures in English - use of of and 's

There is no absolute rule to tell you whether you need to use, or can use, a possessive form with "**of**", on one with "**'s**". The commonly repeated "rule" that you can "only use 's with people" is quite wrong. It is a very broad generalisation, and there are lots of exceptions. Besides, there are a lot of cases where, even with people, you cannot use **'s**.

2.8.1. Animates: human possessors, or assimilated:

2.8.1.1.

In cases of true possession: **'s** is normal. In many cases it will be essential.

> A1 The lady's car wouldn't start.
> A2 The dog's ball was red..

With qualities, attributes or actions: **'s** is common.

> A3 Madonna's reputation is international.
> A4 The dog's name was Jackson.
> A5 The Queen's arrival was delayed.

These can also be easily expressed using **of**.

> A31 The reputation of Madonna is international.
> A41 The name of the dog was Jackson.

There is a **<u>difference in emphasis</u>** between the two alternatives: examples:

- A3-A5 emphasize the <u>possessor</u>,
- A31 and A41 emphasize the <u>quality or attribute</u>.

 In A5, the "possessor" is the subject of the verbal noun (*arrival*) following it
Situations in which there is <u>no</u> choice:
Sometimes, even though both forms are theoretically possible, the **structure** of a sentence will determine the choice of expression, as a word may **<u>have to</u>** stand next to other words qualifying it: for example:

> A32 The reputation of Madonna, the American singer, is international

We can **NOT** say:

> A32X ~~** Madonna's reputation, the American singer, is international. **~~

Examples A1 and A2 must be rephrased using "**of**" if this is structurally **essential**:

> A 11 The car of the lady I had lunch with wouldn't start
> Clearly, the other theoretical option gives the wrong meaning!
>   A 11x ~~**The lady's car I had lunch with wouldn't start. **~~

2.8.1.2. Possessive adjectives:

There is no choice when possession is indicated by a possessive adjective, such as *his, my, your,* etc.

> A61   Your loss is my gain.
> A62   I took my brother to see our grandfather.
>   A 62x ~~I took the brother of me to see the grandfather of us.~~

2.8.1.3. Relating *a part* to a *whole* (animates)

 Use of "of" is **obligatory** when expressing the relation of **a proportion to a composite whole.**

> A71   the **rest of the people,**
> A72   the **majority of voters.**
> A73   a **quarter of the committee**

We can NOT say:

> A71x: ~~the people's rest,~~
> A72x: ~~the voters' majority~~
> A73x: ~~the committee's quarter~~

Of and **'s** are both possible (depending on sentence structure) when expressing the relation of **a part to a unitary (**single**) whole.**

> A8 The **man's arm** was broken, *or*
> A81 The **arm of the man** was broken

2.8.1.4 *: Singular **nouns ending in s**. There are two possible ways to use these in the **'s** possessive form. Compare two examples: **Saint James's Park** is a park in London, but **Saint James' Park** is a famous football stadium in Newcastle. Both names are correct.

2.8.2. Inanimate possessors

For qualities, attributes, actions, or parts: **Of** is the **usual** structure, but **'s** may be possible;

The unusual "'**s**" form can be used with <u>some familiar</u> nouns for stress, or for reasons of sentence structure.

B1	The cost of the operation was enormous.
B2	The condition of the goods we received was not very satisfactory.
B3	The launch of the new book was very successful.
B31	The new **book's** launch was very successful.
B4	Where's the lid of the saucepan?
B5	The front end of the car was smashed up.
B51	The **car's** front end was smashed up.
B6	The departure of the train was delayed for an hour.
B61	The **train's** departure was delayed for an hour.

In examples B3 and B6, where the attribute that is "possessed" is a verbal noun, the sentence could be rephrased using subject and verb instead of the possessive structures.

B32	The **new book was launched** very successfully (subj. + passive verb).
B62	The **train departed** an hour later than planned (subj. + active verb).

2.8.2.1. Relating a part to a whole (inanimates) or a group to its constituents

The **of** form is normally obligatory when expressing the relation of a **part** to a **whole** (or **a whole** to its **parts**) when the part has no meaning except in relation to the whole.

B7	The **top of** the **stairs**.
	(i.e. the word **top** is meaningless without reference to **stairs.**)
B8	The **back of** the **building**
B9	The **middle of** the **report**

The same is usually true when expressing the relation of a **unit** to a **group** (or **a group to its units**) when the group is defined by the units of which it is composed.

B10	A **collection of paintings**
B11	A **group of trees**

We can **NOT** say:

B71x:	~~the stairs' top~~.
B81x:	~~the building's back.~~
B101x	~~A paintings' collection~~

However there sometimes **<u>is</u> a choice** when the part is expressed as adjective+noun, or when the part is more important in the phrase than the whole (B 13, B131),

B12	The top floor of the building
B121	The building's top floor
B 13	The roof of the building was on fire
B 131	The building's roof was on fire.

2.8.2.2. Complemental noun groups

Of is essential, except in a few specific cases.

C1 The theory of relativity	*NOT:* ~~the relativity's theory~~
C2 The Department of Linguistics	*NOT:* ~~the Linguistics's department~~

Complemental noun groups can often be rephrased as **<u>compounds</u>**, *without* 's:

C11 the relativity theory
C21 the Linguistics Department

2.9. Adjectives

An **adjective** is a word that **defines, qualifies or modifies** the meaning of a **noun**, or more rarely of a **pronoun**. It expresses a quality or attribute of the word it qualifies. There are two main categories of adjectives: determining adjectives, and descriptive adjectives, which can be either **qualifying** adjectives or **classifying** adjectives.

2.9.1. Determining adjectives

Also called limiting adjectives, determining adjectives are words that are generally classed in the family of determiners, and are dealt with elsewhere: there is a limited number of these words. They are notably possessive adjectives (such as *my, their*), numerals and quantifiers (such as *one, two, three, every, many*), demonstrative adjectives (such as *this* or *that*), interrogative adjectives (such as *which*). For information on the use of these determining adjectives, consult the appropriate paragraphs.

2.9.2. Descriptive adjectives: qualifying or classifying

When we talk of adjectives, what we generally tend to think of are "descriptive adjectives". These are adjectives such as *big, English, wonderful*, words that describe the permanent or perceived qualities of a noun; their number is unlimited. New descriptive adjectives enter the language every day, often in the fertile world of slang.

There are two categories of descriptive adjectives;

- **qualifying or qualificative adjectives** , such as *big, nice, complicated* which express the passing or perceived qualities of a noun, and
- **classifying adjectives** (including **absolute adjectives**) such as *married, second, hydraulic, unique, dead* which express permanent qualities or absolutes.

Qualifying adjectives are "**gradable**", i.e. it is possible to graduate their intensity, by the addition of an adverb of degree, such as *very, quite, enough*; most qualifying adjectives can also be put into comparative or superlative forms (*big, bigger, biggest*).

Classifying adjectives cannot normally be graded: a person is either *married* or not, or *dead* or not; he or she cannot be "*very married*", nor "*more dead*" than another person, at least not under normal usage of the words.

That being said, many adjectives can be used *either* as qualifying adjectives, *or* as classifying adjectives, depending on the context. Take the example of the adjective *old*.

Examples

My car is very **old.** (qualifying, with a noun)
He is **old. (**qualifying, with a pronoun)
The **old** computer was much quieter than the **new** model. (classifying)

In the first two examples above, *old* is a perceived quality, and therefore gradable, in the third *old* has an absolute value, with the meaning of *former* or *previous*.

See gradation and comparison of adjectives below.

2.9.3. Use of adjectives: attributive or predicative

Adjectives are used in two main ways; they can either be **attributive** or they can be **predicative**.

2.9.3.1. *Attributive adjectives:*

This is the most common use of adjectives, standing next to a noun in a noun phrase. In English, simple and complex adjectives almost always come **before** the noun.

Examples

The **big metal** box
My **dear old** grandfather.
A very **modern plastic** dish.
An easily **recognisable** face.
A **pink and green** dress
A **not-too-infrequent** event.

Exceptions: adjectives that follow nouns or pronouns. (postpositive adjectives)

There are only a very small number of exceptions,

    a)   A few adjectives such as *concerned involved, present* and *responsible*, which have a particular meaning when they come after a noun.

    b)   Some adjectives, notably participles, which can follow a noun when they stand as the contraction of an unexpressed relative clause. (examples 3 & 4)

c) Adjectives that qualify pronouns (examples 5 & 6) must follow.

d) Adjectives of dimension or duration, such as *old* and *tall,* follow the noun in some cases, notably when used predicatively. (ex. 7 & 8)

e) The other important case when an adjective will follow a noun is when the adjective is postmodified by a prepositional phrase. (examples 9 & 10)

Examples

1. All the people **concerned** were told to leave the room.
2. The children **present** did not like the show. (=The children *who were present* ....)
3. He's the last man **standing**.
4. There are only three cakes **left**.
5. I want to give you something **special.**
6. That would be quite understandable to anyone **intelligent**.
7. The man is **seven feet tall** and I'm **20 years old**.
8. There's **a foot deep** hole in the road, and it's **six feet long.**
9. I bought all the bottles **left** in the shop.
10. He was a man **proud** of his success

For details on the ordering of adjectives within a noun group, see adjective order below.

2.9.3.2. Predicative adjectives

Adjectives are said to be **predicative** when they are used as the complement of the verb **to be,** or other similar verbs such as *get, become, grow,* as in these examples.

The result was **magnificent**.
My girlfriend is **beautiful**.
The weather is getting **colder**.
I grew **fonder** of London after living there for a month.

2.9.4. Adjectives in the plural

In English, adjectives **never** take a plural inflexion **(s)** whether they are used attributively or predicatively, for example.

Twelve **good** men…. ***Never*** Twelve ~~goods~~ men

The same rule applies to some **adjectives used as nouns.**

We talk about **the poor**, or **the living**, or **the wounded**. We cannot say ~~the poors~~ or ~~the livings~~, or ~~the woundeds~~.

Example

> **The injured** and **the dead** were evacuated by ambulance.

On the other hand, with **colors**, specially when referring to teams, adjectives used as nouns do take a plural **s** .

Example

> The final is between **the reds** and **the blues**.

2.9.5. Formation of adjectives

Many adjectives are lexical words in their own right, i.e. they exist independently of any other word, or are the root word of a word family. For example *good, bad, ugly*. Other adjectives are inflected forms of other words, derived notably from verbs. For example *charming, lost*. Other adjectives can be formed from nouns, for example *beautiful* (from *beauty*) or *motionless* (*from motion*), or even from other adjectives (for example *yellowish*).

One of the beauties of the English language is the simplicity with which words can be formed from other words: all that is needed is to add the appropriate prefix or suffix, and a new word is made. Here are some examples.

> Unthinkable, doable, mendable, possible, plausible - with -*able* or -*ible*
> Careless, fruitless, homeless, motionless - with *less*
> Beautiful, hopeful, wonderful, awful, blissful - with *ful*
> Soggy, foggy, lazy, stormy, skinny, bloody, - with -*y*
> Smallish, greenish, darkish, - with -*ish*
> Distinguished, bored, displaced, contented, squared - with -*ed*
> Challenging, alarming, amazing, exciting - with -*ing*

2.9.6. Comparison of adjectives

Many qualifying adjectives can be used in a **comparative** or a **superlative** form. In most cases, the comparative form of an adjective is made with the word *more*, and the superlative form with the word *most*.

But with most common short monosyllabic adjectives, and some two-syllable adjectives, the comparative is made by adding the ending -*er,* and the superlative with the ending -*est*. There are two common adjectives with irregular comparative and superlative forms: *good, better, best*, and *bad, worse, worst*.

Examples

Careful, more careful, most careful

Difficult, more difficult, most difficult

Certain, more certain, most certain

Hard, harder, hardest,

Black, blacker, blackest,

Old, older, oldest,

Clever, cleverer, cleverest

Large, larger, largest (just add -r and -st to adjectives ending in e)

Big, bigger, biggest, hot, hotter, hottest -

   Final **p t k b d g n** & **m**, are doubled when standing *alone after a short vowel*

Hard, harder, **warm** warmer, **quiet** quieter -

   Final **p t k b d g n** & **m**, are **not** doubled when *following another consonant or a long vowel or diphthong.*

Pretty, prettier, prettiest , heavy, heavier, heaviest

   Adjectives ending in **y** have inflected forms in **-ier** and **-iest**.

2.9.7. Gradation of adjectives

Qualifying adjectives can be graded by **adverbs of intensity** or of degree, and by some other adverbs. The most common adverbs of intensity are: *quite, rather, fairly, very, extremely, highly .*

These adverbs come before the adjective. But note the following points:

- **Enough**: qualifying an adjective, *enough* comes, exceptionally, <u>after</u> the word it qualifies (examples 6 and 7). (Qualifying a <u>noun</u>, *enough* comes <u>before</u> the word it qualifies).

- **Rather** and **quite**. used attributively, *quite* and *rather* can either follow the article, or come before the article: i.e. we can choose between *a rather good book* and *rather a good book*, or *quite a nice guy* and *a quite nice guy*. With **rather**, the choice is generally open, with **quite** it is more usual to say *quite a* than *a quite.*

Adjectives that are in the comparative form can be modified by intensifiers such as *much, far* and sometimes by adverbs of degree (examples 8). Some kinds of adjectives, notably participles, can be modified by a wide range of adverbs (examples 9 and 10).

1. I'm quite certain I left my hat in the car.
2. This is a rather good movie OR this is rather a good movie.
3. It's very clear that you have read the book already.
4. This is a highly complicated situation to be in.
5. This situation is highly complicated.
6. OK, that was a clear enough reply.
7. Is the door wide enough to get through?
8. That was much better than last time. It's rather better than I expected.
9. They are a newly married couple.
10. He made a carefully worded statement.

Classifying adjectives can not normally be graded, though there are some circumstances where grading is possible. Compare the three examples below using the classifying adjective *electric*. Normally something is *electric* or it is *not electric*; it can't be *very electric* nor *quite electric*...... However it can be *mainly electric*.

Examples

OK: This new car is electric.
Not OK: ~~This new car is **very** electric.~~
OK. This new hybrid car is **mainly** electric.

2.9.8. The order of adjectives

How is it that native English speakers naturally place adjectives (and secondary nouns acting as adjectives) in the "correct" order when writing or speaking? Very few native English speakers have ever learned, or even thought of, the rules that determine the order in which adjectives are placed. This obviously means that the rules are a) very basic and intuitive, and b) very few in number. More than rules, they are conventions.

Adjectives are placed in English according to their nature or type. There are **three groups** of adjectives, defining the qualities of a noun:

> **A. A**rticles **& a**ccessories, relative or perceived circumstantial qualities.

At the start of group **A** come **A**rticles and determiners

> **B. B**asic, permanent but circumstantial qualities

> **C. C**lassifying adjectives, innate or **fundamental permanent qualities**

And of course, they will be placed in the natural order **ABC**, with **the most fundamental adjectives coming closest to the noun, i.e.** last. **Each group** contains different types of adjectives, which may (or may not) require a specific sequence.

This is illustrated in the following table:

Group A	Group B	Group C	Noun
Articles and accessories	**Basic**	**Classifying**	
Article or determiner > **P**erceived quality, > **S**ize, weight, age etc.	**color** > **N**ationality > **G**ender (sometimes gender before nationality)	Permanent quality > substance (often a secondary noun)	
An attractive ancient	**B**ritish	**c**opper	**necklace**
My first big	green	rubber	ball
His five old	American		cousins.
	British female		voters
Magnificent old	American	Ford	automobile.
Memorable	French	skiing	trip
Dangerous and useless		chemical	experiment
Nice fresh	red Spanish		tomatoes

Important! When two group A adjectives of similar nature qualify the same noun, they **may** be linked by *and*. However *and* is **never** required to link adjectives from different groups.

If two adjectives before a **plural** noun are joined by *and*, the phrase may imply two different categories, though a certain ambiguity will often remain, as in: *Attractive and valuable old books can be bought online.*

3 Other parts of speech

3.1. Adverbs

3.1.1. Two families of adverb

There are two main families of adverb:

1.   Adverbs related to or derived from adjectives or prepositions.
2.   Adverbs unrelated to adjectives or prepositions.

Adverbs from either category may fulfil identical functions in the sentence. Each category includes adverbs of four main types: time, place, manner and degree.

Category 1:

    1. **Time:** (duration, sequence): presently, previously, fast
    2. **Place:** (position or direction): locally, closely, upwards, nearby
    3. **Manner:** Quickly, easily, consequently
    4. **Degree:** Extremely, generally, highly, nearly

Category 2:

    1. **Time:** (duration, sequence): already, soon, tomorrow, next
    2. **Place:** (position or direction): Here, there, somewhere, away
    3. **Manner:** too, thus, therefore
    4. **Degree:** very, quite

To understand how "sentence adverbs" (see below) such as *therefore* or *thus* are adverbs like the others (and not conjunctions), just consider that *therefore* is a synonym of consequently, and that *thus* can be a synonym of accordingly.

3.1.1.1. Function of adverbs

Whereas adjectives are used to qualify a noun, **adverbs** are used to qualify a verb, an adjective, or another adverb. Some adverbs - called "sentence adverbs" - can also qualify a whole sentence (see § 3.1.4. below).

3.1.2. Adverbs related to adjectives

Most adverbs in English are related to adjectives; for example *high* (adjective) and *highly* (adverb).

Adjectives	Adverbs	
Qualifying a noun	qualifying a verb	qualifying an adjective
A high mountain	I think highly of you	That is highly improbable
A real surprise	He really likes you	You are really nice.
A fast train	It went very fast	This is a fast moving situation.
In actual fact	I actually laughed	
A bitter disappointment	I bitterly regret saying that.	A bitterly cold day

3.1.2.1 Formation of adverbs

As the examples above show, many adverbs are formed by adding the ending **-ly** to an adjective. Adverbs can be formed from many adjectives in this manner; that includes many participles.

Examples: (adjective / adverb) new / newly, continuous / continuously, recent / recently,
Adjectives ending in -*ful* form adverbs ending in -*fully*: careful / carefully,
Adjectives ending in -*y* form adverbs ending in -*ily*: happy / happily,

Participial adjectives:
Surprising / surprisingly, disgusting / disgustingly, decided / decidedly
There are a few exceptions to this principle.

A few adverbs (and related adjectives) are formed by adding the endings -**ward(s), ways** or -**wise** to nouns or prepositions.

Clockwise , counter-clockwise, sideways, sidewards, forwards, inwards, upwards, skywards etc.

Words in -wise can share the same form as adverbs or adjectives; adverbs ending in -wards normally lose the final **s** when used as adjectives.

A clockwise rotation, a sidewise movement
….in an upward(s) direction, a forward motion

Finally, note that the normal adverb corresponding to the adjective **good** is **well**, not goodly.

3.1.2.2. Adjectives and adverbs with *identical forms*

Here are the eight most common adjective/adverb pairs that share identical forms:

Adjectives	Adverbs	Notes:
A **fast** train	It went very **fast**	
A **hard** day	**He works hard.**	**hardly** also exists - but the meaning is different. *He hardly works* is virtually the opposite of *he works hard.*
A **late** reply	He's working **late**.	**lately** also exists - but the meaning is different.
A **long** day	I **long** thought he'd never return.	**long**, adverb, has the meaning of *for a long time.*
The **Daily** Mirror	We check it **daily**.	
A **monthly** bill	I pay it **monthly.**	
The **wrong** answer	We went **wrong**.	**wrongly** also exists - but with a different meaning.
The **next** day	Who's going **next**?	

Short and long. The adverb phrases **for long** and **for short** are used with specific meanings, and **short**, following a quantity, means "*less than needed / expected*".

I won't be working in London **for long**. (= *for a long time*)
He's called Archibald, but we call him Archie **for short.** (= *because it is shorter).*
When we counted up the bottles, we found that we were seven **short.** (= *we had seven less than expected*).

3.1.2.3. Comparatives and superlatives:

Adjective and adverbial forms are also identical when adjectives are in a comparative or superlative form – unless this is formed with *more* or *most*:

Examples: (adjective / adverb)
   better / better, fastest / fastest, more recent / more recently,
   There was a bright flash / The light was shining brightly
   I need a brighter light / The sun shone brighter (more brightly) in
   the evening.

3.1.3. Adverbs unrelated to adjectives

There are many common adverbs in English that are not related to adjectives; they can be found in all four types, as illustrated above. These adverbs include some important groups:

- Several common adverbs of frequency: **sometimes, seldom, often** etc.
- Several common adverbs of degree: **quite, very, too, enough**
- A number of "Sentence adverbs" , which qualify whole clauses or sentences. (see § 3.1.4 below)

While these adverbs are themselves unrelated to adjectives, they often have synonyms that *are* formed from adjectives.

Examples

Do you come here **often**?
   (**Often** is a synonym of **frequently**)
This is a **seldom**-performed opera by Wagner.
   (**seldom** is a synonym of **rarely**)
We **sometimes** go to the cinema on Fridays.
   (**sometimes** is a synonym of **occasionally**)
You are **quite** sure, aren't you?
Your dissertation is **not** good **enough**.

Important: note that enough, as an adverb of degree, follows the adjective it is qualifying.

3.1.3.1. For the relative adverb **however**, see § 2.4.3.

3.1.4. Sentence adverbs

Adverbs qualifying a whole clause or a whole sentence

Some adverbs can apply (or in some cases only apply) to a whole sentence or statement. These can be:

- adverbs formed from adjectives, including modal adverbs, such as *consequently, possibly, clearly, inevitably, naturally, obviously, surprisingly, fortunately*, or

- other modal adverbs such as *maybe, even, just,* or
- **conjunctive adverbs** such as *therefore, perhaps, so, nevertheless, also...* For more on this see **Conjunctive adverbs.** (§ 3.4.)

To understand how **sentence adverbs** such as **therefore** or **perhaps** are adverbs like the others, just consider that **therefore** is a synonym of **consequently**, or that **perhaps** can be a synonym of **possibly.** Sentence adverbs are not conjunctions (like *but and for* or *as*), since conjunctions must come at the start of their clause; the position of sentence adverbs is not fixed, and they may be put at **different places** in the clause – though not in all cases.

Examples

Clearly you have not understood what I am saying.

You have clearly not understood what I am saying.

Maybe you have not understood what I am saying.

You have maybe not understood what I am saying.

It's snowing, therefore (consequently) the match has been canceled.

It's snowing, the match has therefore (consequently) been canceled.

We will obviously try to find the right answer.

Naturally, you will have to buy a ticket before you leave.

You will have, naturally, to buy a ticket before you go in.

3.2. Prepositions

> **Definition**
>
> A preposition is a short word, for example **at, in** or **by**, that is most commonly used to show the relation between two nouns, two pronouns, or a noun and a pronoun. There are less than forty common prepositions in English.

Prepositions and prepositional adverbs

Many **prepositions** have related adverbs. This section looks at prepositions *and* at the adverbs that are related to prepositions, known as prepositional adverbs.

- **Prepositions** generally **precede the noun** they are referring to, but this is not always the case. They can – indeed sometimes they must – come at **the end of a sentence**, notably in some relative clauses with omission of who, or in some questions.
- **Prepositional adverbs** stand alone; there is no second noun or pronoun.
  Examples

> **Prepositions**:
>   The Queen is **at** home. Dinner is **on** the table. Go **to** bed.
> **Prepositional adverbs**:
>   They're standing **outside**. We're going **together**.

- For prepositions with verbs, see prepositional verbs (§ 1.18)

3.2.1. Prepositions of position and of direction

The table below lists the common English prepositions of position and of direction, and the related adverbs for each case. Many English prepositions can signify either direction or position; but this is not the case for all prepositions.

Prepositions of position and direction normally only introduce nouns or pronouns; a few, such as **into**, can occasionally introduce verb phrases. In this table, less common forms and rarely used equivalents are shown in brackets (--).

Denoting **position**		Denoting **direction**	
Adverbs	**Prepositions**	**Prepositions**	**Adverbs**
	across	across	
	at	at, to [1]	
* in, inside, (within)	in, inside, within	into	in, inwards
outside	outside	(out), out of [2]	out, outwards
(on)	on	on, onto	(on)
	(far from)	from	
overhead	over, above [3]	over (above)	(overhead)
underneath	under, (underneath)	under, (underneath)	
throughout	throughout	through	
below	below	below	
		up	upwards
		down	downwards
nearby	near	(nearer)	
(alongside)	alongside	along	along
in between	between	(between)	
opposite	opposite		

Examples

<table>
<tr><td colspan="2">

Prepositions of position:

    Our friends live just **across** the street.

    I live **in** London.

    There are people **inside** the house.

    He lives **within** a mile of the airport.

    Our apartment is **opposite** the bank.

    There are problems **throughout** the programme.

Prepositions of movement:

    Please put all those bits **into** the box.

    He walked **through** the town.

    The child threw his plate **onto** the floor.

</td></tr>
</table>

Adverbs of position:
 We're staying **in** tonight.   There's someone **inside**!
 Our friends live **nearby**.
Adverbs of movement:
 I can't manage to put this nail **in**.
 Look, now it's moving **inwards** and **downwards**.

Prepositions before a verb phrase:

He tricked me **into** paying far too much.

There are several other types of adverb, many of them derived from adjectives. ▶ For more on this, see Adverbs above (§ 3.1.)

Notes:

1. As prepositions of direction, "**at**" and "**to**" are <u>not</u> synonyms. "At" is not common as a preposition of direction, and is only used with the meaning of *towards* or *in the direction of*, and then only in some contexts. Compare these two sentences.
 I threw the ball to John.   I threw a cup at John.
You can say I'm going to London next week,
but it is impossible to say: "~~I'm going at London next week.~~"

2. In classic English, "**out of**" is the normal preposition of direction.
  Example: *I went **out of** the house.*
But increasingly, particularly in spoken English, the **of** is being dropped, so you are likely to hear: *I went **out** the house.*

3. There is a small difference between "**over**" and "**above**" as prepositions of position. **Above** means *over, but not touching.*
So you could say *There are clouds above London,*
but it would be strange to say *There is fog above London.*

3.2.2. Prepositions of time

English has nine common prepositions of time. Except for the word since, which is used as a preposition and as an adverb, there is either a choice of corresponding adverbs, or no corresponding adverb.

Prepositions	Adverbs
before	before, beforehand, before that, earlier, previously
after	after, afterwards, then, later, subsequently
by	
in	
at	whereat, (thereat), whereupon
since	since
for	
during	meanwhile
until	

Examples: prepositions and adverbs of time

I'm playing football **before** lunch; but **earlier** I have an English lesson.
I'm playing football **before** lunch; but **before that** I have an English lesson
He goes to Chicago **after** Detroit; **afterwards** he's going to Minneapolis.
The package must arrive **by** the end of the week / .... **by** Friday.
I'm leaving **in** five minutes. / I like going to England **in** the summer.
Everyone applauded **at** the end of the concert.
Online ticket sales began **at** 8 a.m, **whereupon** the whole program
   crashed.
I've lived in London **since** the start of 1995 / .... **since** my childhood. [1]
She went to Australia 20 years ago, and we haven't seen her **since**.
I'm going to New York **for** a week in the summer
He worked in Dubai **for** three years. / ... **for** many years. [2]
During his vacation, he won $ 3000 on the Kentucky Derby.[3]
He's getting a new apartment tomorrow; **meanwhile** he's staying in a hotel
   until Friday.

Notes:

1. **Since** is used with moments in time, or with units of time, but not with numeric quantities. We cannot say ~~since three weeks~~. **Since** can also be used as an adverb, with no following noun, and often strengthened with ever, as in:

He moved to San Francisco in 2000, and he's been there ever since.

2. **For** is used with **numerals** (or undefined quantities).

3. **During** is used with **periods** of time; it is not used before numerals.

4. **Prepositions of time** cannot introduce verb phrases. When before, after, since and until are used in front of verb phrases, they are functioning as **conjunctions**, not as prepositions;

Before coming to London, he.... is the same as *Before he came to London, he…*

For more on For and since see the Linguapress online grammar.

3.2.3. Other Prepositions - manner and other relations

English has eight common prepositions of manner, relation or agent:
against, among, by, for, of, with, without, except.
For full details about the use of **of**, see *§ 2.8 Possession*, above.

Examples

> The Dallas Cowboys are playing **against** the Miami Dolphins next week.
> He was just one **among** many candidates.
> The Harry Potter books were written **by** J.K.Rowling.
> I've just bought a present **for** my mother.
> I'm going to Florida next week **with** my girlfriend.
> You can't play football **without** a ball.
> I told everyone **except** my brother.

3.2.3.1 *As used as a preposition*

Another word that may be used as a preposition is **as**, with the meaning of *in the condition of* or *in the role of,* or as in many common idioms on the model *as (adjective)… as (noun).*   For **as** as a conjunction, see § 3.3.2.

Examples

> I'd like to think of you **as** a friend.
> That's really not too bad **as** a first attempt.
> **As** an adult, you ought to set a good example.
> It's **as** light **as** a feather.

3.2.3.2 *Prepositions introducing a verb phrase:*

> He broke his glasses **by** standing on them.
> You can't play football **without** using a ball.

Note that **by** and **without**, in the last two examples above, are effectively being used **prepositions** and not as **conjunctions**.

While we **can** say

   OK   *Before coming to London... or Before he came to London....*
      We **cannot** say

  Not OK   *He broke his glasses by he stood on them.*

By is never used as a conjunction.

3.2.4. And a few more prepositions

Apart from these common prepositions, English has several more words or phrases that can be used as prepositions.

A few examples: **Apart from, following, amid, via, per.**

3.2.5. Ending a sentence with a preposition; is it OK?

Simple answer: **yes**! Lots of great writers have done so. Sometimes it may be better style to put the preposition in its normal place, before the noun, if this is possible; yet sometimes this is not possible or practical and a "*dangling preposition*", left on its own at the end of a sentence or clause, will be the best solution.

Look at these examples:

1. This is the talented young musician I was talking to you **about**.
2. What are you waiting **for**?

In these contexts – example 1 being a relative clause with omission of the relative pronoun, and example 2 a question requiring a preposition - it is perfectly good, indeed often **the best solution** possible in modern English, to leave the preposition at the end of the sentence.

The alternatives, without a *dangling preposition* are either rather formal (example1) or very archaic and formal (example 2), and should be avoided.

1. This is the talented young musician **about whom** I was talking to you.
2. **For what** are you waiting?

3.3. Conjunctions and connectors

- The **four categories of connector** , which are explained below, are
    - coordinating conjunctions, such as **and** or **or**,
    - subordinating conjunctions such as **if, so that, because** or **while**. and
    - correlating conjunctions such as **neither... nor**
    - conjunctive adverbs such as **therefore** or **however**
- A small number of conjunctions and conjunctive adverbs can link individual words or phrases; but the majority can only link two clauses.
- A coordinated clause or phrase **must** follow the clause or phrase to which it is connected.
- A subordinate clause **normally** follows the main clause, but in some cases may precede it. See below.
- In most cases the difference between subordination and coordination is clear, but in some cases linguists disagree.
- A subordinate clause cannot stand alone: it needs a main clause to complete the sentence.

3.3.1. Conjunctions

3.3.1.1. Coordinating conjunctions

Coordinating conjunctions are used to link two clauses or phrases or words of equal value or equal status. There are only a small number of coordinating conjunctions in English: most sources repeat what others say, and list the following seven, using the convenient acronym FANBOYS.

- for, and, nor, but, or, yet and so.

This is a popular but misleading mnemonic. So forget fanboys, forget for and so, and go for the acronym BANYO.

- For can be forgotten, as it is hardly ever used as a coordinating conjunction in modern English. It has been replaced by because or as.... which are clearly subordinators.
- As for so, grammar books and websites provide contradictory and often ambiguous information. *So* let's clarify the situation.

When **so** implies **purpose** it is clearly a subordinating conjunction. The subordinate clause can come before or after the main clause.

> **OK** I bought a new camera **so** I could take better pictures.
> OK **So** I could take better pictures, I bought a new camera.

When **so** implies **consequence** linguists disagree as to whether it is a coordinator a subordinator. But either way, the **so** clause must **follow** the main clause.

> OK I bought a new camera **so** I took better pictures.
> **NOT OK** ~~So I took better pictures, I bought a new camera~~.

Many online dictionaries and grammar books do not distinguish coherently between the usage of **so** for purpose and **so** for consequence, or are very ambiguous on this point.

And and **or** can link individual words or clauses; **yet** and **but** normally only link clauses, but sometimes link two words. **Nor** cannot link words when it is a coordinating conjunction it can only do so in partnership with *neither*, as a correlative conjunction.

Usage:

Coordinating connectors give equal value to the two elements that they coordinate. They **must** be placed **between** the two elements that they coordinate.

Examples

> I want three beers **and** a glass of lemonade.
> He went to bed **and** went to sleep.
> You can have the chocolate mousse **or** the lemon tart
> They'll win, **or** they'll lose.
> This present is not for Peter, **but** for Paul.
> I bought a new dress that was not red **but** pink.
> We're going to Paris, **but** not to Rome.
> We're going to Paris, **but** we're also going to Rome.
> He was very tired **yet** very happy.
> The director was rather young, **yet** the company was successful.

3.3.1.1 Can you start a sentence with a conjunction?

A lot of grammar books claim that it is wrong to start a sentence with a conjunction. This is just **not true** ! And never has been.
Most of the great writers in the English language have used sentences starting with conjunctions. In the "King James" version of the Bible, which was the standard work of reference for style in the English language for three centuries, two of the first three sentences in the first chapter of the book of Genesis start with **And**.... These initial "ands" remain present in the main modern 20th or 21st century versions of the Bible, including the Contemporary English Version (CEV) and the American Standard Version (ASV).

> *In the beginning God created the heaven and the earth.*
> ***And*** *the earth was without form, and void;* ***and*** *darkness was upon the face of the deep.*
> ***And*** *the Spirit of God moved upon the face of the waters.*

So yes, you **can** start a sentence with a conjunction.

3.3.2. Subordinating conjunctions

Subordinating conjunctions are used to link two clauses within a single sentence, when one clause is **subordinate to** the other. In other words, the subordinate clause clarifies, expands or explains the meaning of the main clause.

Some types of subordinate clause are introduced by **subordinating conjunctions**, others (such as relative clauses) are not. Common subordinating conjunctions include

- **as , because** and **since** (cause)
- **so** and **so that** (purpose)
- **although** and **though** (contrastive)
- **after, before, until, while,** etc. (temporal)
- **if, unless, as long as, provided, whenever, whatever** (conditional, indirect question)
- **that** (reported speech, indirect statement, consequential)

Usage

Subordinating conjunctions must come at the **start of the subordinate clause**.
There are two sorts of subordinate clauses.

1. **Most subordinate clauses** can come either **before or after** the main clause. So unlike coordinating conjunctions, subordinating conjunctions can stand at the start of a sentence.

2. But **indirect questions, relative clauses**, and subordinate clauses introduced by **that**, must normally be placed **after** the main clause, just like a coordinated clause *(Examples 12, 16 and 17)*

3.3.2.1. Examples of subordinating conjunctions

In these examples, it is **not possible to invert** the two clauses in sentences **written in blue (12, 16 & 17).**

1. I 'm going to London because I've got a new job.
2. Since it's raining, I'm going to watch a movie this afternoon.
3. She didn't want any more wine, as she'd already drunk enough.
4. As she'd drunk enough, she didn't take any more wine.
5. I'm locking the door, so nobody can get in.
6. So he wouldn't forget to wake up, he set his alarm for 5.30.
7. Although I love him, I wouldn't want to marry him.
8. This book is good, though some bits of it are rather boring.
9. After I finished work, I went straight home.
10. Until they opened a new factory, they could not produce enough.
11. If you see anything suspicious, let me know at once.
12. He asked the policeman **if** he knew of a good restaurant.
13. Provided you can swim, you can come out on our yacht.
14. You can come out on our yacht, as long as you can swim.
15. I won't go there, whatever he says.
16. This ice-cream is so good, **that** I'm going to have another one.
17. The man said **that** he was born in New York.

3.3.2.2. So as a subordinating conjunction

So is a **subordinating conjunction** when it is used to denote a **purpose**. A *so* clause denoting purpose does not usually come before the main clause, but it is not impossible *(example 6 above).* When **so** is used to indicate **consequence**, i.e. with the meaning of *therefore* or *and similarly*, it is a **conjunctive adverb**.

3.3.3. Correlating coordinators

These can either correlate words, or phrases, or clauses (sentences).
The main examples are:

> **both.... and, not only.... but also,** (combining correlators)
> **either...or , whether.... or not** (binary choice correlators)
> **neither.... nor,** (negative correlators)

Other correlating pairs include:

> **the more..... the more.....**
>
> **no sooner..... than...**
>
> **hardly ... than**

and a few other expressions. Note also that **many adjectives** can be used in their comparative form, preceded by **the**, as circumstantial correlating coordinators, as in.

> **The higher** they rise, **the harder** they fall.
> **The sooner** you stop doing that, **the better** (it will be).

Usage

When it is **words** or **phrases** that are coordinated, the coordinator normally has to precede the element it is correlating.

When **clauses** are correlated, the coordinators generally precede each correlated clause, but this is not always the case, as illustrated in examples 5 and 6 below .

Examples

1. This is **both** stupid **and** incomprehensible.
2. **Both** the president **and** the prime minister were there.
3. I can understand **both** his reasons **and** his arguments.
4. **Not only** can I hear him, **but also** I can see him
5. I can **not only** hear him, **but also** see him.
6. **Not only** can I hear him, I can see him (too).
7. I bought **not only** some blue suede shoes, **but also** a big cowboy hat.
8. It's **either** right **or** wrong.
9. **Either** it's right, **or** it's wrong
10. **Either** Mommy **or** Daddy will pick you up after school.
11. I'll go there **whether or not** I'm allowed to.

12. I'll go there **whether** I'm allowed to **or not**.
13. We're going home now, **whether** you like it **or not**.
14. **Neither** Paul **nor** Mary could come to my party.
15. I'm **neither** angry **nor** happy.
16. I **neither** like that man, **nor** dislike him
17. **I neither like that man; nor do I dislike him.**
18. I have **never** been to Florida on vacation; **nor** have I been there on business.
19. **The more** you earn, **the more** you spend.
20. **No sooner** *had I* opened the door, **than** the phone rang.
21. **Hardly** *had the plane* taken off, **than** the pilot reported some trouble.

Notes

- **Both ... and** can correlate words, and occasionally clauses (Examples 1 - 3)

- When **not only** <u>**starts**</u> a clause, the verb and subject of the first clause are inverted. (Example 4).

- **But also** can be omitted, after **not only** (Example 6).

- When **nor** introduces a clause, subject and auxiliary/modal verb are inverted. (Examples 16 - 18).

- **Neither** can be replaced by **not** or **never** in the first of two correlated clauses. (Example 18).

- When **no sooner** or **hardly** introduce clauses, auxiliary and subject are inverted. (Examples 20 & 21)

- For other uses of **whether**, see *Conditional clauses with whether* § 1.5.6. above.

3.4. Conjunctive adverbs

Conjunctive adverbs such as however or therefore

3.4.1. The nature of conjunctive adverbs:

> **Definition**:
> **Conjunctive adverbs**, which are a type of discourse marker, belong to the family of words known as *connectors*; they are a type of *sentence adverb* used in order to express a particular relationship between a first clause and a second clause that **follows**. In most cases, the two clauses will be separated by a semi-colon (;).

Conjunctive adverbs are very similar to **subordinating conjunctions**. The biggest difference is that conjunctive adverbs can frequently (but not always) be used in **a variety of positions** within the subordinate clause, whereas subordinating conjunctions **MUST** stand at the start of the subordinate clause.

Examples

> **Conjunctive adverb**: example **however** - *the position in the clause is flexible*
> * They bought a new car; it was **however** still too small for their family.
> * They bought a new car; it was still too small for their family, **however.**
> * They bought a new car; **however** it was still too small for their family.
> They bought a new car; it was still too small **however** for their family.
> **Subordinating conjunction**; example **although** - *only one position is possible.*
> * **Although** they bought a new car, it was still too small for their family.

Conjunctive adverbs express different relationships between two clauses: for example

Addition - also, besides, moreover,

Consequence - consequently, hence, so, therefore, thus,

Comparison – similarly, likewise,

Contrast – alternatively, if not, however, nevertheless, otherwise,

Confirmation - indeed, of course, naturally

Clarification - for example, for instance, namely, i.e.

In most cases, a conjunctive adverb will come **at the start** of the clause that it introduces; however this is not essential, and with many conjunctive adverbs **other positions** are possible.

More examples

They played some music by the Beatles; **also / additionally** they did some songs by Elvis.

They played some music by the Beatles; they **also / additionally** did some songs by Elvis.

Let's buy that one, it's quite nice; **besides**, it's not expensive either.

He's one of the directors; **consequently (hence, so)** he gets a BMW and a free parking space.

He's one of the directors; he **consequently** (*but not* hence *nor* so) gets a BMW and a free parking space.

You should have seen the doctor by now; **if not** you should make an appointment.

You should have seen the doctor by now; you should make an appointment **if not**.

Yes I loved that cocktail; **nevertheless** I won't have another one, thankyou!

Yes I loved that cocktail; I won't have another one, **however**!

The best students will all get prizes; **certainly** you'll be one of them.

The best students will all get prizes; you'll **certainly** be one of them.

You need to work less; **i.e.** you should take a vacation (*no other position is possible with* **i.e.**).

You need to work less; you should take a vacation **for example** (*the position of* for example *may be flexible*).

3.4.2. Usage

While they are both "connectors", It is important to distinguish between **conjunctive adverbs** and **subordinating conjunctions**, as they are not used in the same way. There are differences at two levels – the **position of the secondary clause** within the sentence, and the **position of the connector** within the secondary clause, as the next table shows.

Secondary clause.....	With a **conjunctive adverb**	With a **subordinating conjunction**
Examples	*Also, however, therefore, in fact, nevertheless, moreover,* *so* (meaning *therefore* or *and the same is true for*)	*Although, as, because, before, until, while, since,* *so** (in the sense of purpose), *so that*
Position of the **secondary clause** in the **sentence**	**Fixed**: **It must follow** the main clause	It can either precede or follow the main clause
Position of the **connector** (adverb or conjunction) within its **clause**.	Often **flexible**	**Fixed**: It must come at the **start** of the secondary clause

The case of too

Too means the same as **also**, but is used **after** the clause to which it applies *(examples 15 and 16 below)*. **Too** can also be used as an intensifier at the end of a secondary clause introduced by **and.**

Different meanings of so

So, as a conjunctive adverb, can either express

- a **consequence** (*see example 5*) or

- an **additional action** (*see example 6*).

When **so**, is used to introduce an additional action, it is necessary to invert the subject and the auxiliary. The same goes for the negative equivalent of **so**, which is **nor**. (*Examples 6 & 7 below*).

For **so** with the meaning of purpose, see **so** on Linguapress online grammar. Linguapress.com/grammar/.

Conjunctive adverbs in use.

More **Examples:**

<table>
<tr><td>1.</td><td>I bought a new shirt; I **also** bought some new shoes.</td></tr>
<tr><td>2.</td><td>I bought a new shirt; **also** I bought some new shoes.</td></tr>
<tr><td>3.</td><td>I bought a new shirt; I bought some blue suede shoes **also.**</td></tr>
<tr><td>4.</td><td>This is good cheese; **besides** it's made locally.</td></tr>
<tr><td>5.</td><td>There's no more beer, **so** we'll have to drink lemonade.</td></tr>
<tr><td>6.</td><td>I went to San Francisco last summer; **so** did my brother.</td></tr>
<tr><td>7.</td><td>I didn't go to San Francisco, **nor** did my brother.</td></tr>
<tr><td>8.</td><td>They won the state lottery, **therefore** they are now rather rich.</td></tr>
<tr><td>9.</td><td>He found the solution; **thus** he was able to finish the project in time.</td></tr>
<tr><td>10.</td><td>He found the solution; he was **thus** able to finish the project in time.</td></tr>
<tr><td>11.</td><td>You can cross by ferry; **alternatively** you can take the Channel Tunnel.</td></tr>
<tr><td>12.</td><td>They bought a new house; it was **however** still too small for their family.</td></tr>
<tr><td>13.</td><td>They bought a new house; it was still too small for their family, **however**.</td></tr>
<tr><td>14.</td><td>Stop making that noise, **otherwise** I'll call the police.</td></tr>
<tr><td>15.</td><td>John went to London; Mary went there **too.**</td></tr>
<tr><td>16.</td><td>I saw John and Mary **too.**</td></tr>
</table>

4 Sentences and clauses

4.1. Word order in statements

> **A color-coded guide to English word-order**
>
> In the examples below, parts of the sentence are color-coded: subjects in red, verbs in blue, direct objects in maroon, etc.

The man put the book on the table.

Tomorrow they're going to Miami.

Indeed he often gave the cat some milk.

4.1.1. Subject and verb

▶ **4.1.1.1.** In a normal (declarative) sentence, the subject comes directly in front of the verb which is normally the first element of the predicate. The **direct object** (when there is one) comes directly after it:

Examples

> The man wrote a letter.
> People who live in glasshouses shouldn't throw stones.
> The president laughed.

▶ **4.1.1.2.** Note that by **the subject,** we mean not just a single word, but the subject noun or pronoun plus adjectives or descriptive phrases that go with it. The rest of the sentence - i.e. the part that is not the subject - is called the predicate.

Examples

> People who live in glasshouses shouldn't throw stones.
> I like playing football with my friends in the park.
> The child who had been sleeping all day woke up.

▶ 4.1.2. Other parts of the sentence

If a sentence has any other parts to it - indirect objects, adverbs or adverb phrases - these *usually* come in specific places:

4.1.2.1 The indirect object

The **indirect object** <u>follows</u> the **direct object** when it is formed with the preposition *to*:

The **indirect object** <u>comes in front of</u> the direct object if *to* is omitted.

Examples

> The doctor gave **some medicine** **to the child**.
>
>   or: The doctor gave **the child** **some medicine.**

4.1.2.2. Adverbs or adverb phrases

Adverbs (single words) and **adverb phrases** (groups of words, usually formed starting with a preposition) can come in three possible places.

1) **Before the subject** (Notably with short common adverbs or adverb phrases, or sentence adverbs - *see below*).

Examples

> **Yesterday the man** wrote a letter.
> **At the end of March the weather** was rather cold.
> **Obviously the man** has written a letter.

2) **After the object** (virtually any adverb or adverb phrase can be placed here), **or**, with intransitive verbs, **after the verb.**

Examples

> The man wrote **a letter** **on his computer in the coffee shop**.
> The child **was sleeping** **on a chair in the kitchen**.

3) Or in **the middle of the verb group** (notably with short common adverbs of time or frequency).

> The man **has already written** his letter.
> The new version of the book **will completely replace** the old one.
>
> You **can sometimes get** real bargains in this store.

4.1.2.3. Word order with *"sentence adverbs"*

Sentence adverbs (like *perhaps, surely, indeed, naturally, also ....*) relate to a whole clause or sentence, not just a single word. In most cases, they stand outside the clause they refer to, notably at the start of the clause. However, they may be placed elsewhere in the clause for reasons of stress or emphasis.

Examples

> Surely the man has already written his letter.
> Perhaps the man has already written his letter.
> The man has perhaps already written his letter
> ..., therefore the man had already written his letter.
> Naturally the man grew vegetables in his garden.
> > *Contrast this with:*
> > The man grew vegetables naturally in his garden.
> > *which has a quite different meaning.*

For more details, see § 3.1.4. Sentence adverbs.

4.1.2.4. Subject and verb, verb and object

In standard English, nothing usually comes between the subject and the verb, or between the verb and the object.

  There are a few exceptions. The most important of these concern *adverbs of frequency* and indirect objects without to. (Examples 1 and 2 below)

  Adverbs of frequency will normally be placed in the middle of the verb group when the verb consists of more than one word. (Example 3)

Examples

> 1. The man *often* wrote his mother a letter.
> 2. I *sometimes* have given my dog a bone.
> 3. I have *sometimes* given my dog a bone.

The examples above are deliberately simple - but the rules can be applied even to complex sentences, with subordinate and coordinated clauses.

Example

> The boss, [who *often* told *his staff* (*to work* harder),] *never* left the
>   office before (he had checked his email.)

Exceptions

Of course, there are exceptions to many rules, and writers and speakers sometimes use different or unusual word order for special effects. But if we concentrate on the exceptions, we may forget the main principles, and the question of word order may start to seem very complex!

So here are just a few examples of exceptional word order: you should realize that they exist, but **not** try to use them unless either they are essential in the context, or else you have fully mastered normal word order patterns. (Don't try to run before you can walk!)

A few examples of exceptional word order:

Never before had I seen such a magnificent exhibition.
> <u>After</u> *never* or *never before*, subject and verb **can** be - and usually are - inverted. Do not invert when never <u>follows</u> the subject!.

Hardly had I left the house, than it started to rain.
> When a sentence starts with *hardly*, subject and verb **must** be inverted.

Had I known, I'd never have gone there.
> Inversion occurs in unfulfilled hypothetical conditional structures when *if* is omitted. See § 1.5. on conditional clauses for more details.

The book that you gave me I'd read already.
> Emphasising a long object; in this example *The book that you gave me*, is placed at the start of the sentence for reasons of style: this unusual sentence structure is not necessary, just stylistic.

4.1.3. Complex or compound sentences.

Generally speaking, the order of words in the clauses of compound sentences follows the general principles of word order as explained above. For specific cases see

> § 1.5 Conditional clauses,

> § 3.3. Conjunctions and connectors,

> § 4.3. Reported questions,

> § 4.6. Relative clauses.

4.2. Word order in questions

How to form correctly ordered questions in English

Making correctly-formed questions in English is really **so simple**.... Almost all questions use the same structure. All you need to do is to remember this simple and common English phrase:

How **do you do**?

The structure of <u>almost every simple question</u> in English is based on this same model:

   (Question word if there is one) - Auxiliary or modal - subject - main verb - (plus the rest of the sentence):

4.2.1. Question words - or wh- words

In English there are three types of question word

- **Interrogative pronouns** - who, whom, whose, what, which
- **Interrogative determiners** - which, what or whose (followed by a noun),
- **Interrogative adverbs** - where, why, how etc.

Examples

Where did Mark Twain live?

Whose is that car?

Did Arnold Schwarzenegger learn English quickly?

How quickly did Arnold Schwarzenegger learn English?

Has the bank sent us an invoice yet?

How many books have you read this year?

Is the new secretary being given her own laptop?

Can the new secretary be given her own laptop?

How quickly can the new secretary be given her own laptop?

Is the new secretary nice?

Why can't we have a second chance?

Important: *take care!*

In the interrogative, as in the negative, English verbs are **ALWAYS** made up of at least two elements, an auxiliary and the root verb.

In the interrogative there is <u>only one</u> exception to this rule, and that is certain tenses of the verb to be, as in example 2 above.

Examples:

> **Are** you ready?
>
> **Is** that true?
>
> **Were** they already at the pub when you got there?

For **all other verbs** - including **to have** - tenses that are formed with a single verb in an affirmative statement (i.e. the present simple and the simple past) are formed in the interrogative by the addition of the auxiliary **do**.

4.2.1.1. Modal verbs

Note that with **modal verbs** except *have to*, **do** is **not added** in order to form a question. The modal itself is the first verb unit. *Have to* is the only basic modal verb to which **do** needs to be used as the first verb in order to form a question.

Examples:

> **Can** you **tell** me the time, please?
>
> **Should** that child **be crossing** the road without an adult?
>
> **Must** you **make** such a noise?
>
> **Do** you **have to make** such a noise !

4.2.2. Statements and questions with single-word tenses

> He had a good time. > **Did he have** a good time?
>
>   NOT ~~Had he a good time~~?
>
> He lives in New York. > **Does he live** in New York?
>
>   NOT ~~Lives he in New York~~?

4.2.3. Exceptions

Certain **adverbs**, notably short adverbs of frequency or time, can and indeed sometimes must be placed **between** the **auxiliary** and the **root verb**, as in statements. In questions, these adverbs are placed between the subject and the root verb.

> **Has** that Chicago company **yet sent** us their order?
>
> **Can** the new secretary **soon be given** a bigger desk?
>
> **What sort of hats** do the ladies **usually wear**?

4.3. Reported questions

Reported questions and verb tenses in English

While expressing reported *statements* in English is relatively easy to master, putting direct *questions* into reported speech can often cause problems for the learner.

The simplest way to master the rules or structures is to start with a few varied direct questions, and use them as models. We will use the following Models:

> ► M1. Where is my jacket? (question using *to be*)
> ► M2. What is making that noise? (*Wh* word as subject,)
> ► M3 Does she like chocolate? (no question word present)
> ► M4. What are you doing? (*Wh* word as object).
> ► M5. Where do you live? (*Wh* word as adverb).

Preliminary points:

a) The main thing to remember is that in reported interrogatives, there is no inversion of subject and verb.

b) Reported speech can be introduced by a lot of different verbs, but most commonly by expressions such as "*He asked...... , I wonder.....*" etc.

When there is no **question word** (as in model M3), indirect questions are introduced by *if* or *whether.* See below.

4.3.1. Reporting the present: simultaneous reporting.

This is not complicated. The verb tense in the reported question is the **same** as in the original question.

M1. "Where is my jacket?" ► *He's asking where his jacket is.*

M2. "What is making that noise?" ► *I wonder what's making that noise*

M3. "Does she like chocolate?" ► *I wonder if (whether) she likes chocolate.*

M4. "What are you doing?" ► *He's asking what you're doing.*

M4. "What is he saying?" ► *I wonder what he's saying.*

M5 "Where does he come from?" *I wonder where he comes from.*

4.3.2. Reporting the past: deferred reporting

This is a little more complicated, but not impossible to master. It is the more common form of reporting. The verb in the reported question usually changes.

4.3.2.1. Reporting the past from the *present*.

If the reported question refers to a past situation, the verb in the reported question clause should go in the **past**. But if the reported question refers to a permanent or ongoing situation (**M11, M21,** etc.) , it *can* remain in the present.

M1." Where is my jacket ?" ▶ *He asked where his jacket **was**.*

M11 "Where is London ?" ▶ *He asked where London **is.***

M2. "What is making that noise ?" ▶ *I wondered what **was** making the noise.*

M21 "Who lives in this house ?" ▶ *I wondered who **lives** in this house.*

M3. "Do you want a chocolate?" ▶ *They asked (me) If I **wanted** a chocolate.*

M31 "Do you speak English ?" ▶ *He asked (me) if I **speak** English.*

M4. "What are you doing ?" ▶ *He asked what you **were** doing.*

M41 "What are you doing ?" ▶ *He asked what you**'re** doing.*

M4. "What is he saying?" ▶ *I asked what he **was** saying.*

M5. "Where does he come from ?" ▶ *I asked him where he came from.*

In the examples above, the *jacket* (M1) has moved since the question was asked, but *London* (M11) has not moved. We can suppose that the *noise* (M2) has stopped, but that the person *still lives* (M21) in the house, and so on.

As for example M31, people often put the verb into the past tense in this type of reported question, though strictly this is not necessary, nor really correct. "*He asked me if I spoke English*" suggests that speaking English is something you can do one day, but not the next..

4.3.2.2. Reporting what was the *future* in the original question.

When a direct question using a **future** verb form is reported, the future form of the question clause becomes a conditional, or a future-in-the-past when what *was* the future is now the past.

*will > **would**   –   are going to > **were** going to – can > **could**, etc.*

If the original future is **still** in the future (M11, M31, etc.), then the reported question remains in the future.

M1.	"Where will you be **tomorrow**?" ▶ *He asked **where I would be** the following day*.	
M11	"Where will I be in 2050 ?" ▶ *I wondered where **I'll** be in 2050.*	
M2.	"What will come next ?" ▶ *He asked what **would come next***	
M3.	"Will you take me home?" ▶ *I asked if he**'d take** me home .*	
M31	" Will he still be there in 2050 ?" ▶ *I wondered if he'll still be there in 2050.*	
M4.	" What are you going to do ?" ▶ *He asked what I **was** going to do*	
M41	"Who's she going to marry ?" ▶ *They asked who she's going to marry.*	
M5.	"How will you survive?" ▶ *He asked me how I'd survive .*	

4.3.3. Absolute and relative adverbs of time or place

English (like many other languages) has a series of adverbs of time and place which are *absolute* concepts, and strictly related to present time (the moment) or place. *Now, today, yesterday, tomorrow, in five minutes' time (etc.), here.*

In indirect questions or statements, the moment is not normally the same as it was when the question or statement was originally made. Therefore it is often necessary to change the adverb of time (or place) and use one that expresses a *relative* concept of time (or place). Here are the most common pairs:

- Today   ▶ *that day, on the day….*
- Tomorrow   ▶ *the next day, the following day*
- Yesterday   ▶ *the day before, the previous day*
- Now   ▶ *then, at that moment,*
- In five minutes' (etc.) time   ▶ *five minutes (etc.) later*
- Here   ▶ *there*

Example:

"Can you be here tomorrow?" would be reported as:
        *He asked if I could be **there** the following day.*

4.4. Tag questions

What are tag questions, and when are they used?

4.4.1. Definition and function

Tag questions - also referred to as **question tags** - are very common, particularly in spoken English. They are short interrogative tags that can be added to the end of a declarative statement. Tags are usually added to a statement in order to express *opinion, possibility* or *probability*. Although they use an interrogative structure, tags are **not** real questions. They are **requests for confirmation.**.. or sometimes for contradiction.

4.4.2. Tag structures

4.4.2.1. Normal structure of tags

 Question tags are normally formed on the model **verb > pronoun subject**. They are placed at the end of the sentence or clause. Using a standard interrogative inversion, they repeat the auxiliary used with the main verb and the pronoun corresponding to the subject of the main verb, as in these simple examples.

That man is reading a good book, **isn't he**?
Those students have passed their exams, **haven't they**?
They didn't go to San Diego last week, **did they**?

a). Standard tags

 In standard tags, it is important to note that there is always an **opposition** between **affirmation** and **negation**. If the main verb is in the affirmative, the tag will be in the negative: conversely, if the main verb is in the negative, the tag will be in the affirmative.

That lady **is** reading a good book, **isn't she**?
Those students **haven't** passed their exams, **have they**?

b). "True-question" tags

 Occasionally, but not often, speakers use "same-way tags", or "true-question" tags where there is **no opposition** between affirmation and negation. They are normally used in affirmative contexts: in this case both the main verb *and* the tag are in the affirmative. The speaker is either really asking for an answer, or else expressing doubt about the truth of the statement.

> **Examples**
> That lady **is** reading a good book, **is she**?
>   Meaning either: *Is that lady actually reading a good book?*
>   or: *I am really questioning whether that is a good book; I don't think so.*
> Those students **have** passed their exams, **have they**?
>   Meaning: *Have those students really passed their exams? That's*
>   *surprising.*

It is important to remember that "same-way tags", or "true-question" tags are not common. It is useful to know that they exist, and what they mean; but students of English are best advised not to use them unless they are really sure that they understand the nuances or implications.

4.4.3. Use of tags

Tags are placed at the end of a statement or sentence; they are formed by repeating the auxiliary (*be, have, do* - **examples 1-6**) or the modal auxiliary (*can, must, might* etc. **examples 7 - 12**) used with the main verb, followed by a pronoun corresponding to the subject of the main verb. As stated above, there is normally an **affirmative/negative contrast** between the main verb and the tag.

Examples

> 1.   The Queen of England's over 90, **isn't she**?
> 2.   Those new shoes weren't very expensive, **were they**?
> 3.   You've remembered all the instructions, **haven't you**?
> 4.   The kids hadn't had anything to eat, **had they**?
> 5.   You did remember to turn off the gas, **didn't you**?
> 6.   The secretary didn't like the new boss, **did she**?
> 7.   He can sing quite well, **can't he**?
> 8.   You can't come to the concert tonight, **can you**?
> 9.   We shouldn't continue without the guide, **should we**?
> 10.   You really ought to get permission first, **oughtn't you**?
> 11.   You couldn't understand anything he said, **could you**?
> 12.   The students really have to work hard, **don't they**? *

Note the last example above: tags following the **modal auxiliary** "*have to*" (as opposed to the **past auxiliary** *have*) are forms of the auxiliary *do*, not *have*, even if the main verb is in the affirmative.

If the main verb does not use an auxiliary (i.e. it is in the simple present or simple past tense), the tag will be formed using a form of the auxiliary *do*, just like the interrogative and negative forms of these tenses.

Examples

The President lives in the White House, **doesn't he**?
Those new shoes look very expensive, **don't they**?
You remembered all the instructions, **didn't you**?
This one looks rather interesting, **doesn't it.**
People who eat too much **get** fat, **don't they**?

Note the last example above: the tag reflects the **main verb** of the sentence of course; *get* not *eat*.

If the main verb is accompanied by several auxiliaries, including modal auxiliaries, the tag reflects back to the **first** of the auxiliaries used.

Examples

The President **might** have been in the White House, **mightn't he**?
You **should** have been paying more attention, **shouldn't you**?
They **could** have lost all their money in Las Vegas, **couldn't they**?
He ought to have been able to answer all the questions, **oughtn't he**?
He might have had to buy a new computer, **mightn't he**?
They can't have had to stop already, **can they**?

Used with reported speech and similar structures, it is important to remember that the tag reflects the **main verb** of the sentence, not the verb of the reported speech.

He **said** you were very clever, **didn't he**?

It **looks** like we ought to be getting out of here quickly, **doesn't it?**

They **didn't think** it was particularly easy, **did they**?

The judge **believes** that the accused is innocent, **doesn't he**?

You **were telling** us about what you did in Quebec, **weren't you**?

You **don't think** there's anything wrong with my idea, **do you**?

4.4.4. Uncontracted negative tags

Just occasionally people express negative tags without contracting the word **NOT** to **n't**.

IMPORTANT! In uncontracted tags, the word order is different, as **NOT** follows the verb: Compare the following:

This point has already been clearly explained, **has it not**?

It's good, isn't it / It's good, **is it not**?

They're very late, aren't they / They're very late, **are they not**?

You've seen the show, haven't you /

You've seen the show, **have you not**?

Uncontracted tags are used particularly in written English, where the contracted form might seem too informal. They are also used in some dialects, or by speakers wishing to sound more formal.

4.5. Negative structures

Different ways of expressing negation in English

4.5.1. Negative forms of the verb

In most cases a negative meaning is given to a **verb** by adding the negative
verbal particle **NOT**. In some cases, **not** is replaced by **never**.

 Not (sometimes shortened to **n't**) normally follows the principal auxiliary or
modal verb in a verbal structure. In the few cases where there is no
auxiliary or modal (present simple or past simple affirmative tenses), it
follows a reconstituted auxiliary, *do* or *did*. The choice between **not** and **n't**
is a matter of style. **Not** is generally preferred in written English, **n't** in
spoken English

Examples

> He lives in San Francisco / He **does not** live in San Francisco.
> I can see you / I **cannot** see you / I can't see you.
> I like those photos / I **don't like** any of those photos.
> The man lost all his money / The man **did not** lose all his money.
> I should eat (some) more chocolate / I **shouldn't** eat (any) more
> chocolate.
> You ought to have gone home / You **ought not to** have gone home.
> I may be able to finish in time / I **may not** be able to finish in time.

Never is used in the same way as **not**, except when the verb is in the simple present or simple past tense. With **never**, there is no need to add a missing auxiliary using a form of do.

Examples

> He plays tennis / He **never** plays tennis. (*but not* ~~He does never play~~)
> I saw the President yesterday / I **never** saw the President yesterday.
> I've been to England. / I've **never** been to England.
> You should eat a lot of chocolate / You should **never** eat a lot of chocolate.
> You ought to have done that / You ought **never** to have done that.
> I may be able to finish this. / I may **never** be able to finish this.

See also pages on *to have* (§ 1.12) for **important distinctions** between the different forms of the negative with to **have** as a **main verb** or as an **auxiliary**. (Specifically, when to use **haven't** and when to use **don't have**, for example).

4.5.2. Negating a quantifier

The particle **not** can also be added to the quantifiers **much** or **many**, to form the small-quantity quantifiers **not much** or **not many**. It can also be added to **enough**, to give the meaning of *insufficient quantity.*

Examples

> **Not many** people came to the concert last night.
> It's still pretty poor, and **not much** better than it used to be.
> **Not enough** people bought tickets, so the show was cancelled.

4.5.3. Negation using a noun or pronoun

Less frequently, a negative meaning may be implied by attaching a **negative particle** to a **noun** group, either the subject or the direct object of a sentence. In this case, the negative particle that is used is **no**. **No** is sometimes combined with *-one, -thing, -where,* etc. to make negative indefinite pronouns, **no one, nobody, nothing, nowhere**, etc.

Examples

Trees grow on the moon   / **No** trees grow on the moon.

I can see someone   / I **cannot** see anyone / I can see **no one.**

The man lost time / The man lost **no** time

I should eat more chocolate / I should eat **no** more chocolate.

There's something in that box / There's **nothing** in that box.

The riders were able to finish the race/ **No** riders were able to finish the race.

None of is used in the same way as **no**, except that it is followed by a definite article, another determiner, or a pronoun. When only two people / items are concerned, **none** is normally replaced by **neither**.

Examples

The riders were able to finish the race **/** **None of** the riders were able to finish the race.

Your shoes are clean **/** **None of** your shoes are clean.

I like those photos / I like **none of** those photos.

Did you eat some chocolates? / Did you eat **none of** the chocolates?

In the event, **none of** us were right, all three of us were wrong.

In the event, **neither of** us were right, we were both wrong.

For more on negation with nouns, see § 2.6. Some and Any as quantifiers.

4.5.4. Negation using an adverb phrase

It is also possible to add a negative meaning to a **sentence**, by including an **adverb phrase with a negative meaning**. The most common group of negative adverbial phrases are formed using the word **without**, or a preposition followed by **no**.

Examples

You can have some whisky / You can **do without** whisky.   He's walking with a stick / He's walking **without a stick**   He did it for a good reason / He did it for **no** reason at all.   I want you to do it with me /   I want you to do it **without** me.

4.5.5. Neither and nor - linking two negative statements

Neither and **nor** are used to link a pair of negative pronouncements. **Nor** can be used by itself to introduce the second of a pair of negative statements, even if a normal **not** structure is used in the first one. **Neither** and **nor** can be attached to verbs, or to nouns (subjects or objects), or even to prepositional phrases.

When **nor** introduces a **second main clause**, the subject and the auxiliary or modal are **inverted**. See examples 3 to 5 below.

Examples

1.	He **neither** looks like a gentleman, **nor** talks like a gentleman.
2.	I can **neither** see it **nor** hear it.
3.	I didn't agree with what he said. **Nor did I** believe him.
4.	He hasn't eaten for three days; **nor has he** slept.
5.	They can't find the problem; **nor can they** explain why it happened.
6.	I like **neither** your appearance **nor** your attitude.
7.	**Neither** the President **nor** the Secretary of State was (were) present.
8.	I could convince him **neither** with my arguments **nor** with my warnings.
9.	You should wash this in water, but **neither** with soap **nor** with detergent.

4.5.6. Negation using negative adjectives

An affirmative statement can be turned into a negative statement by adding a **negative prefix or suffix** to an appropriate adjective.

Examples

This is possible > This is **im**possible.
You are being very cooperative > You are being very **un**cooperative.

The border guards were friendly > The border guards were **un**friendly.

I'm very pleased with my results > I'm very **dis**pleased with my results.

He's being very sensible > He's being very sense**less.**

4.5.7. Negation with tag questions

Negative **tags** attached to the end of affirmative statements have the structure and appearance of negative questions, but they do not really express a negative value, and they are not really questions; they are essentially an expression of minor doubt, or a means of requesting confirmation of a statement or an opinion.

▶ For more on this, see Tag questions (§ 4.4.) above.

4.6. Relative clauses

Forms and functions of relative clauses in English grammar

> This page looks at standard **relative clauses**, using the principal relative pronouns *who that* and *which*.
> For information on *nominal relative clauses*, and on other relative pronouns or adjectives such as *whatever* or *when* or *whenever*, ▶ see Relative pronouns (§ 2.4.2.)

Relative clauses can cause trouble in English, specially when they begin with less common forms of the pronoun *who*, such as "whom" or "whose". And there's another problem: when to use **which** and when to use **that**? This topic is dealt with in nine parts.

4.6.1. Clauses with the relative pronoun as subject

4.6.2. Clauses with the relative pronoun as object and the question of whom

4.6.3. The relative pronoun as a possessive

4.6.4. Relative clauses starting with a preposition

4.6.5. More complex structures

4.6.6. Restrictive and non-restrictive relatives, and punctuation.

4.6.7. Using that

4.6.8. Relative clauses which qualify a whole sentence, not just a noun.

4.6.9. Omission of the relative pronoun.

4.6.1. Clauses with the relative pronoun as subject

1.1. When the relative pronoun is **subject** of a clause and refers to a **human**, the relative pronoun *who* is generally used.

Examples

> The man **who** lives next door is 99.
> I know someone **who** eats red hot chilli peppers.

Sometimes, **who** is replaced by **that**, especially in American English and in spoken language:

Examples

> The boy **that** lost his watch was careless.
> *However ...*

> The boy **who** lost his watch was careless.   *is also quite possible.*
> *After the antecedent **those**, who *or* that *can be used*
> Those **who** can swim should go first.
> Those **that** can swim should go first.

1.2. If the relative is the **subject** of a clause and refers to an **inanimate** antecedent, *which* or *that* must be used.

Examples

> The book **that**'s on the table is mine.
> The book **which** is on the table is mine.

1.3. IMPORTANT

Omission: As <u>**subject**</u> of a clause, the relative pronoun <u>**can never be omitted.**</u> However, the relative clause can be completely omitted.

> **Examples**
> ~~*The book **is** on the table is mine*~~ *is quite impossible, but*
>   The book on the table is mine   *is perfectly acceptable.*

4.6.2. Clauses with the relative pronoun as object

Even if the relative pronoun is the object of the clause, it still stands **at the start** of the clause.

4.6.2.1. When the relative pronoun is the **direct object** of the clause, and refers to a **human**, the pronoun used is either *whom* or *that*.

Examples

> The man *whom* I saw yesterday is 99.
>   The man *that* I saw yesterday is 99.

Omission: when it is the object of the relative clause, the relative pronoun can often be omitted, in both spoken and written styles.

>   The *man I saw* yesterday is 99.

The relative, whether mentioned or not, is the <u>**only**</u> object of the clause, and there can be no second object following the verb.

Thus we <u>**cannot say or write:**</u>

>   ~~*The man whom I saw him yesterday is 99*~~.
>
>   nor   ~~*The man I saw him yesterday is 99.*~~

The question of whom

Whom is not used very often: *that*, or omission of the relative pronoun, are much more common. In spoken English, **whom** is going out of use as an object pronoun, replaced by **that** or omitted entirely. In direct questions, it is usually replaced by **who** in spoken English except in very formal style.

Examples

> **Whom** did meet last night ? *sounds very formal.*
> *Most speakers would ask:*   **Who** did you meet last night?

4.6.2.2.   When the relative pronoun is the **direct object** of the clause, and refers to **an *inanimate object*** , the pronoun used is *which* or *that*.

> The book *that* I was reading was very interesting,
> *or* The book *which* I was reading was very interesting,
> *or* The ***book I was reading*** was very interesting.

4.6.3. The relative pronoun as a possessive

Whose is required with both animate and inanimate antecedents: it is the only derivative of *who* which can refer to animates *and* inanimates.

Examples

> I know someone **whose** sister is a nurse.
> The man **whose** car I borrowed is very rich.
> I chose the set **whose** price was reduced.

4.6.4. Relative clauses starting with a preposition

Note how to form relative clauses after prepositions: we use **preposition + which** for inanimates or things, **preposition + whom** for people. Stylistically, this is quite formal.

 When referring to places or locations (but **not** to objects), **in which** is often replaced by *where*; when referring to a moment in time **in which / at which** is sometimes replaced by *when.* (See also § 2.4.2.4 above).

Examples

> The man **with whom** I was talking was angry.
> The chair **on which** he sat down collapsed.
> In the town **where / in which** I was born …
> The room **in which** / ~~where~~ I was sitting …
> Describe the moment **at which / when** you first became suspicious

4.6.5. More complex structures

Examples

> **1. Preposition + possession:**
> The player **on whose** skills the match most depended, was the kicker.
> It is to my parents, **thanks to whose** generosity I was able to go to
>   college, that I am most grateful.
> **2. Selective possession:**
> The diner, **most of whose** customers had deserted it, had to close.
> The writer, **the first of whose** books had been a bestseller, was a coal
>   miner.
> There are several ways to go from New York to Los Angeles, **the fastest
>   of which** is of course by plane.

4.6.6. Restrictive and non-restrictive relative clauses

A **restrictive** relative clause (also called a **defining** or **integrated** relative clause) is one which is essential for the understanding of a statement. In this case **commas are not required** before and after the relative clause.

Examples

> **Protesters who** smash windows will be arrested.
> **Cars which** can do 150 miles per hour are pointless.
> **Cars that** can do 150 miles per hour are pointless.

The first example tells us that "**protesters who smash windows**" will be arrested; but suggests that those who do **not** smash windows will **not** be arrested. The word "protesters" in this example is restricted by the relative clause that defines it.

In a **non-restrictive** relative clause (also called a **non-defining** relative clause or a **supplementary** relative clause) , the relative clause is **not** essential for an understanding of the sentence. In cases like this, **commas are usually required** before and after the relative clause.

Examples

> **Protesters, who** are mostly aged under 30, want to express an opinion.
> **Cars, that** were invented at the end of the 19th century, have become a
>   vital part of modern life.

In the first of these examples, the question of age is not an essential bit of information. In the second, it is obvious that it is *cars in general*, not cars from the late 19th century, that are a vital part of modern life. The relative clause can be omitted without making the sentence meaningless. Compare these two examples:

Examples

> *1.* **People who eat** too much tend to have poorer health.
> 2. **Sportsmen, who watch** their diet, are not usually over-weight.

4.6.6.1. *One of* + a relative clause

When **one of + group noun** is followed by a relative clause, the **verb** in the relative clause will be in the singular if the relative clause – with or without commas - is non-restrictive (just applies to **one)**, in the plural if it defines **the group.** Take care; some grammar books give wrong information on this point, but choosing either a singular verb or a plural verb is the only way, in this case, of avoiding ambiguity.

Examples

> 1. Just **one** of my friends **who was** **born** in Scotland wears a kilt.
> 2. Just **one** of **my friends who were** **born** in Scotland wears a kilt.

In example 1, only one of these friends was born in Scotland; in example 2 the speaker has several friends who were born in Scotland.

4.6.7. Using **that** instead of **who** or **which** in relative clauses

- The relative pronoun **that** may be used in English, particularly American English, in restrictive relative clauses.
- **That** <u>cannot replace</u> **who** in **non-restrictive** relative clauses.

Examples

> *Protesters,* *who* *(that…no !) are mostly aged under 30, want to express an opinion.*

However use of **that** instead of **who** or **which** in **restrictive clauses** is an **option**, not a rule, and a source of plenty of confusion.

Some grammar books suggest that **which** or **who** *must* be used in restrictive relative clauses, and that **that** *must* be used in non-restrictive relative clauses. This is not correct, neither in American nor British English, and countless quotes from the best authors demonstrate this.

Don't rely on grammar checkers that come with word-processing software.

Experience shows that they are not terribly good at distinguishing **restrictive** from **non-restrictive** relative clauses, and may want to wrongly "correct" a user's punctuation.

4.6.8. Relative clauses which qualify a whole sentence

Sometimes we use a relative clause to qualify not just a noun or pronoun, but a whole sentence or clause. In such cases, the relative clause is introduced by **which**, never by ~~that or what~~.

Examples

He drank too much, **which** is why he was sick.

It was raining yesterday, **which** was a pity.

There aren't enough tables in the exam room, **which** is rather a problem.

4.6.9. Omission of the relative pronoun

See sections ▶ 4.6.1, 4.6.2, and 4.6.4 above.

When the relative pronoun is omitted in a prepositional relative clause (as seen in § 4.6.4)., the **preposition must** come at the end of the clause. This is true even if the end of the clause is also the end of the sentence. This is not a problem. As stated above, omission of the relative pronoun in prepositional relative clauses is **normal style** in modern English. It is sometimes suggested that ending a sentence with a "dangling preposition" is bad style and should be avoided, but in this case, leaving the preposition to the end of the sentence is not just acceptable, it may be essential.

Examples

I hope that this is a page you'll really learn something **from**.

Our company currently has enough financial reserves to get **by with**.

The project our team is currently working **on** is of huge potential
       significance.

4.7. Punctuation

Punctuation is an **essential** (not optional) aspect of written communication in all European languages. Most languages use the same signs and conventions; and while these are used in the same general manner in all languages, they are not used in exactly the same way in all languages. Without punctuation, most texts in written English would be impossible or very hard to understand.

In English there is a certain flexibility over punctuation; and American and British conventions are not identical. Nevertheless there are some clear rules that **must** be followed, either because they are the accepted norm, or because they help to avoid ambiguity or just make a sentence comprehensible. One classic example shows this conclusively! *"Let's eat, Grandma!"* does not mean the same as "*Let's eat Grandma.*" The main rules and conventions are listed below.

Punctuation in written language corresponds to **pauses** and **intonation** in spoken language.

4.7.1. Different types of punctuation

Punctuation is mostly made up of signs , but is also marked by spaces, line-breaks and the capitalisation of some words.

A list of the main punctuation elements in English

- **.** The **period** (American English) or **full stop** (British English)
- **:** The **colon**
- **;** The **semi-colon**
- **,** The **comma**
- **?** The **question mark**
- **!** The **exclamation mark**
- **'** The **apostrophe**
- **—** The **dash**
- **-** The **hyphen**
- **" "** **Quotation marks**, or **Inverted commas**
- **( )** **Brackets**, or **parentheses**

  plus Use of **paragraphs** and **capital letters**

4.7.2. Use of paragraphs

IMPORTANT: The use of paragraphs is one of the most widely ignored rules of good writing, notably by students writing dissertations or essays, or managers writing reports or letters .

Paragraphs divide a long block or text into manageable units. There is no hard and fast rule about when to start a new paragraph; but there are some conventions to follow.

<table>
<tr><td>

Good paragraph practice

Avoid having more than five sentences in a **single paragraph.** Three-sentence paragraphs are just fine.

Start a **new paragraph** when you move to a new idea or a new topic.

A paragraph can contain just a **single** sentence. This is often the case in journalistic style, when writers are trying to express ideas simply and bluntly.

</td></tr>
</table>

4.7.3. The period (or full stop)

- The period (USA) or full stop (GB) is used to separate sentences. In this case, it must be followed by a capital letter.
  - It is also traditionally used at the end of shortened titles, such as **Capt.** , **Prof. Lt.** (Lieutenant), **Cllr.** (Councillor) etc. ; but it is often omitted with **Mr** (or Mr.) (never write *Mister* in full) or **Mrs** (or Mrs.)., and never used after **Miss**.
  - It is used at the end of common abbreviations, such as Mon. (for *Monday*) or etc. (for *etcetera*).
  - It is not required, though occasionally used, for writing acronyms or initials, such as NATO, UNESCO, the USA, the FBI,

Examples

<table>
<tr><td>

Peter arrived in Singapore in January 1996, on his twenty-second birthday. Less than a year later, he had married the boss's daughter Yi Ling.

I'd like you to meet Mr Mark Porter, Miss Elizabeth Taylor, Capt. Eliot Saunders and his wife Mrs Saunders.

I began teaching at UCLA on Mon. 29th Aug. 2018, after five years with UNICEF.

</td></tr>
</table>

4.7.4 The colon

Colons are used to **separate** (a) **two main clauses**, or (b) a **main clause and a phrase**, when the second clause or phrase provides an **example** or an **illustration** of what is said in the first clause.

Examples

I told him what he ought to **do: he** should tell her at once that he'd lost his job. I only like three sorts of **fruit: apples,** pears and bananas.

4.7.5. The semi-colon

- Semi-colons are used to **separate two long main clauses**, when they both have the same subject, and/or are both part of a single topic or idea; they are particularly used when the second clause starts with a conjunction.

- Semi-colons are also used as a kind of "**super comma**", in sentences which have a number of commas, and where one or two breaks need more emphasis than others.

Examples

I had seen lions and rhinoceros in the zoo, most recently at a zoo in **Florida; but** I'd never before seen them in the wild in their natural environment. The students, who'd been there for three days, were sleeping in **tents; as for** the medical staff, they had a bungalow to sleep in. I'd been to England, Scotland, and Wales, which I particularly **enjoyed; and** also to France, Spain, and Portugal.

4.7.6. The comma

Commas are principally used to separate clauses, to put words into relief in a sentence, or to separate elements in a list.

Often the use of commas can be a matter of personal taste or style; however some commas are essential:

1. Commas are **required** with non-restrictive relative clauses (but not with restrictive relative clauses) (See § 4.6.6. above) .
2. Commas (or semi-colons) are **needed** to separate contrasting parts of a sentence, including two short main clauses.

3. Commas are **recommended** in all but very short lists; sometimes they are **essential**, as in example 3b below, which is incomprehensible without them.

4. Commas are **required** at the end of quoted direct speech, when this is followed by words like *he said*, *they told us* or *said the President.*

Examples

1a. Elton John, who is a great pianist, is a campaigner for gay rights.
1b. Scotch Whisky, which has to be imported, is popular in Brazil.
2.   Peter was just getting out of bed, but his wife Mary was already washed dressed and in the car.
3a. Would you please bring me three apples, two bananas, a pear, and a carrot.
3b. You can choose different color-schemes, including black and white, pink and purple, bright orange, and yellow and green.
4a. "I'm a hundred and one years old," the old man said.
4b. "I don't know what you are talking about," answered Jennifer.

4.7.7. The apostrophe

Apostrophes are required in two, and only two, different situations.

- **Possession: before a final s** added to a singular noun, or **after the s** of a plural noun.

- **Omission:** To indicate that a letter or more than one letter has been omitted.

An apostrophe is NEVER required before an s marking a plural.
An apostrophe is not required in the possessive adjective its, only for it's when this is a contraction of it is.

Examples

This is my brother's bicycle.
The manager was very disappointed with the players' poor performance.
Don't go away, it's hard enough with just two of us.

4.7.8. Capital letters

Capital letters are required in a number of different situations:

1. All **proper nouns** (names), and **adjectives formed from proper nouns**, must be capitalized, *unless* the semantic connection between the adjective and the noun has been lost (as in french fries, which are not usually French).

2. Capitals must also be used for **titles**, whether we are talking about human titles (such as *General, Prince*, etc.), or the titles of books, movies etc.

3. Capitals must be used when writing **days of the week, months of the year**, but *not* for the names of the seasons.

4. Capitals must be used throughout **initials** or **acronyms**

5. And finally, of course, every **new sentence** must start with a capital letter.

Examples

> My Brazilian friend from Rio speaks good English, and he loves Italian pasta and German beer; but he never eats potatoes, not even french fries.
>
> General Eisenhower became President of the United States; one of his favourite books was "A Connecticut Yankee in King Arthur's Court".
>
> The campsite is open in the summer months of July and August, and in autumn until the last Sunday in October.
>
> The United Nations has several subsidiary organizations, including UNICEF and UNESCO.
>
> Each new sentence must start with a capital. There are no exceptions to this rule.

4.7.9. Other marks of punctuation

Quotation marks

Quotation marks are required at the start and at the finish of all direct speech, even after a short interruption by a dialogue tag like *he said.*

Question marks

Question marks are required at the end of all direct questions, but are not necessary, and often considered wrong, at the end of indirect questions.

Exclamation marks

Exclamation marks can replace periods at the end of a sentence, to express surprise. Do not over-use them, as this is bad style.

Other punctuation marks

Long dashes can be used, rather like brackets, to put part of a sentence into parentheses, specially if alternative forms of punctuation could lead to ambiguity.

Hyphens are used to form common compound nouns or adjectives, or else to clarify the relationship between words in a noun group. While some common compound words are always hyphenated, in many cases it will be a matter of personal choice.

For detailed rules on the use of hyphens in English, see Rossiter: Problem words in English, section 24.

Examples

> "I was in the garden," he said, "but I didn't see anything."
> "Are you sure?" asked the judge.
> The judge asked if he was sure.
> "Help! "
> Nothing quite so exciting has ever been done before!
> There are three large strange animals — no-one knows exactly what they are — that are sometimes seen on the mountain at night.
> It was a heart-breaking story about a used-car salesman and his daughter-in-law.

4.8. Language and style

Written and oral styles of English

In any language, different styles of expression are appropriate in different situations. We can go from the formal to the informal, the written to the spoken, from technical language (or jargon) to slang.

There are no "rules" as such; nevertheless, there are plenty of features which distinguish **formal** styles from **informal** styles. Here are some of them.

4.8.1. Basic principles of English style

*Note: these are principles or conventions: they are **by no means** to be considered as "rules".*

a) The more **formal** a document is, the more it will use inanimate nouns (i.e. things, processes, ideas, rather than people) as the subjects of sentences.

b) The more **formal** language is, the more it is likely to use **passive** structures (see § 1.8. above: Passives.)

c) The more **formal** language is, the more **verbal nouns** (i.e. nouns like *development* or *creation*) it will use.

d) The more **formal** a document is, the more words of **Latin** origin it will use.

Conversely

a) The more **informal** or spontaneous language is, the more it will use **humans** as the subjects of sentences.

b) The more **informal** a text is, the **less** it will use passive structures,

c) The more **informal** a text is, the more it will use **verb** structures where a choice is possible (i.e. *develop* or *create*) instead of verbal nouns.

b) The more **informal** or spoken a text is, the more words of **Germanic** origin it will use.

From formal to informal, written to spoken English

Here are some **examples**; in each case, **the same idea** is expressed using three different levels of formality: look at the different changes that occur, as we move from a **formal style** via an **intermediate style** and to an **informal one.**

1. The inclement climatic conditions obliged the President to return earlier than scheduled.
The president was obliged to return earlier than planned due to poor weather conditions.
The president had to go back sooner than planned because the weather was so bad.

2. Please await instructions before dispatching items.
Please wait for instructions before sending items off.
Don't send anything off until you're told to.

3. Essential measures should be undertaken at the earliest opportunity.
One should undertake any necessary measures at the earliest opportunity.
You should do whatever you have to as soon as you can.

4. Prior to the discovery of America, potatoes were not consumed in Europe.
Before America was discovered, potatoes were not eaten in Europe.
Before they discovered America, Europeans didn't eat potatoes.

Written and spoken versions of a language use different styles, different registers. To talk in "written English" may be no more appropriate than to write using a "spoken" variety of English. Generally speaking, written English is always more formal than spoken English. Nevertheless, there are informal forms of written English (notably in fiction and in the popular press), and formal styles of spoken English, in particular "discourse", or prepared speech.

Written style can also be affected by the **length** of sentences used, the length of paragraphs, and other features of punctuation.

The same Idea expressed in six different styles:

In the following examples, the same message is expressed in **six** different styles, from an extremely formal written style, to a very informal spoken style. Note in particular how the **color coded word groups** evolve.

In order to demonstrate a full range of styles using a single "message", it is necessary to choose a subject or topic which people actually write or talk about in a whole range of contexts. These examples show the different styles, from the very formal to the informal, that could be used for expressing a message about government fiscal policy (or, to put it less formally, government tax policy). Different parts of the message are color-coded: see how they change from one style to the next.

a) Jargon, very formal.
*This is the style of language used in official reports, technical studies, etc. It is exclusively a style of written English, full of **verbal nouns, technical** words and **passives**.*

♦ Consequent to the <u>appreciation</u> in the exchange value of **the dollar** against other currencies, increased interest rates were introduced by the Federal Reserve in order to <u>reduce the likelihood of</u> an <u>import-led consumer spending surge.</u>

b) Written, formal, clear.
This is clear, written English, as found in the "quality" press or in documents - even on <u>technical subjects</u> - aimed at ordinary educated readers.

♦ *After the international value of **the dollar** <u>rose</u>, the Federal Reserve was obliged to raise interest rates to <u>reduce the likelihood of</u> a <u>surge in consumer spending led by cheaper imports.</u>*

c) Written style for the general public, discourse, scripted radio or TV news style.
This is classic English written style, as found in books, popular newspapers, and magazines for the general public. It is the style of formal discourse – discourse being spoken English from a written or "scripted" text.

♦ As the value **the dollar** <u>increased</u> compared to other currencies, the Fed was forced to put up interest rates to <u>head off</u> <u>a rapid increase in consumer spending spurred on by cheaper imports.</u>

d) Formal spoken style - radio, seminar, talk.

♦As **the dollar's** international value <u>went up</u>, the Fed had to put up the cost of borrowing to <u>head off</u> <u>a consumer spending boom spurred on by cheaper imports.</u>

e) Relaxed, informal spoken style: discussion.

There is plenty of use of **prepositional verbs.** All actions are now expressed through **verbs**, not verbal nouns .

♦ As **the greenback** <u>went up</u> in value, the Fed had to put up the cost of borrowing to <u>stop</u> <u>consumers splashing out on too many cheap imports.</u>

5. A glossary of essential grammar terms

A list of the main terms of grammar

used to describe the words and functions of the English language

A thematic glossary of grammar terms, the words commonly used to describe points of grammar in English. The four lists below cover

1. units of meaning,

2. parts of speech,

3. structural elements and

4. general grammar terms.

The object of these lists is to explain with sufficient detail, yet as succinctly and clearly as possible, the essential vocabulary or "metalanguage" of English grammar.

5.1. Units of meaning (from big to small)

Document: A document is a written, pictural or sometimes oral, presentation of facts, fiction, ideas or opinions. It is or can be considered as complete and comprehensible in its own right.

Paragraph: Paragraphs are the principal sub-divisions of written documents. In standard descriptive or declarative documents, a paragraph is a group of sentences with the same theme. Though there is no rule, grammarians tend to agree that a paragraph will normally have between two and eight sentences, with an optimal length of 3 to 5 sentences. Longer documents may be divided into larger subdivisions such as chapters or sections or even books.

Sentence: A sentence is the basic unit that constitutes a declarative or interrogative statement. With the exception of single-word imperatives or interrogations (such as *Look!* or *What?*) or single-word answers (such as *Me.*), a sentence contains at least two words and consists of a subject and a predicate. A simple sentence contains a single clause. A compound sentence contains more than one clause.

Single word sentences can usually be considered as **ellipses**, i.e. the contraction of a longer sentences. For instance *Look!* really means something like *Look at that* or *Look at me.*

Clause: A clause is a group of words that contains a subject and a predicate. We can distinguish **main clauses**, which can stand as sentences in their own right, and **subordinate clauses** which cannot. Examples:

> Free-standing main clause: *My brother likes fast cars.*

> Two coordinated main clauses: *My brother likes fast cars, but he drives badly.*

> A main clause and a subordinate clause: *He likes cars which can go fast.*

Phrase: A phrase is a group of words which form a single unit of meaning. Examples:

> *The man in the red shirt* is a phrase, but so is *the red shirt* on its own.

Word: A word is the smallest complete <u>free-standing</u> unit of meaning in a language. Words come into several different categories which we call "**parts of speech**". These are detailed below.

Morpheme: A morpheme is the smallest unit of meaning in language. A word may be made up of a single lexical morpheme:

> Examples: *Give / child / speak / good / please*

or of a combination of morphemes, at least one of which must be lexical.

> Examples: *Giving / children / speaker / goodness / nationalistic*

> In the last example, *nation-al-ist-ic*, we can see four morphemes: *nation, al, ist, and ic. Nation* is a lexical morpheme or lexeme, *al ist* and *ic* are functional morphemes that cannot exist on their own, but which when attached to the lexeme serve to change its meaning or function.

A morpheme is not the same as a syllable. The word *nation* is one morpheme but two syllables

5.2. Parts of speech or grammatical categories

These descriptions are deliberately brief. Each of these parts of speech is defined and described in greater detail, with more examples, in the main part of the grammar.

Adjective: (§ 2.9.) An adjective is a word that describes or modifies a noun, or occasionally a pronoun.

Examples: *Good / bad / ugly / disreputable,* as in *A big man / A good one.*

Adverb: (§ 3.1.) An adverb is a word that describes of modifies a verb, an adjective, another adverb, or occasionally a whole sentence.

Examples: *Slowly / generally / upwards / somewhere / quite*

Article: (§ 2.5.) An article is a type of determiner which comes before a noun. In English we distinguish two sorts of articles, the definite article *the*, and the indefinite articles *a* and *an*. Some grammar-books also include the word *some* as an indefinite article.

Conjunction: (§ 3.3) A conjunction or connector is a word that is used to link sentences, clauses, phrases or words. The main examples: *and / but / or / yet*. See Coordination

Noun: (§ 2.1.) A noun is a word that describes an entity (person, item, substance etc.) or a process. It is usually preceded by a determiner (article or other determiner) and may be qualified or modified by one or more adjectives, by prepositional phrases, or by another noun. Nouns are divided into two main categories, count or countable nouns , that can be counted, and non-count or uncountable nouns that cannot.

 Examples: *Man / woman / chair / basket / oxygen / philosophy / idea*

Preposition: (§ 3.2) A ▶preposition is a short functional word that serves to relate two other words in terms of space, time, manner or other relation. Prepositions are essentially used to introduce a prepositional phrase (like *in the beginning*), or to inflect the meaning of a verb (like *to come in*).

Examples: *in / on / under / against / after / with / by*

Pronoun: (§ 2.4.) A pronoun is a (usually) short word that allows a speaker or writer to refer back to an already-mentioned (or implied) noun, or to a statement, without repeating it. The main groups of pronouns are personal pronouns (*I you he she it one we they...* and their object forms or possessive forms, *me, her ...* and *mine, hers*), demonstrative pronouns (*this, that* etc.) and relative and interrogative pronouns (*who, which* etc.).

> **Examples**: *I saw him (him* being a previously mentioned, or implied, male person*).*

> or *Yes, I heard it (it* being a previously mentioned, or implied, object such as *the bell,* event such as *the explosion,* or sentence such as *The bell rang early*).*

Verb: (*§ 1.0*) A verb is a word that describes an action or a state of being. The verb is the key word in a sentence, and no sentence can exist without one. The shortest of all sentences consist of a single verb used in the imperative form. Example: *Look!*

There are two sorts of verbs: *dynamic verbs* describe actions or changes of state: examples *go / become / sit down / move; Stative verbs* describe a condition or state of being: examples *be / like / know.*

5.3. Structural elements of a sentence

Subject: The subject is the main actor or the main topic of a sentence. In a basic declarative sentence, the subject comes before the verb. The subject may be just a single pronoun or noun, such as He or The cat; but in many sentences it is may be quite a bit more, including adjectives, prepositional phrases, relative clauses or more. In this example, all the words in **red** make up the subject.

Example: *The old man in the red shirt who's talking too loudly is my uncle.*

Verb: See *Verb* above.

Predicate: Everything in a sentence that is not the subject. The predicate includes the verb, or verbs, plus any other elements that may be present, notably objects or adverb phrases.

Direct Object: The **direct object** is the entity (person, thing, process) that is directly concerned by the action expressed through the verb, or is the entity that explains the action or process. It is the complement of a **transitive** verb. It can be a pronoun, a noun, a noun phrase, or more than one of these.

> Examples: *I like* **chocolate** */   I like* **them** */ I like* **people who are friendly** */*

> *I like* **people who are friendly and don't smoke cigarettes, including you**.

Indirect object: The **indirect object** is the person or entity that is the recipient of the action, or for whom the action is done. When the indirect object follows the direct object, it is introduced with the preposition *to*; but if it precedes the direct object, *to* is omitted.

> Examples: *I gave a bone **to the dog***
>
> *I gave **the dog** a bone / I gave **it** a bone.*

Main clause: The main clause is the principal clause in a sentence. There can be one main clause or more in a sentence; if there is more than one main clause, these will be separated by a semi-colon (;), or by a coordinating conjunction such as *and, but* or *yet*.

A **subordinate or dependent clause** cannot exist without a main clause. It is normally introduced by a subordinating conjunction, such as *since, if, because* or *as,* or by a relative pronoun such as *who* or *that.*

> Examples: *You can go home now **if you've finished your project.***
>
> ***As I said,** there are no tickets left for the concert.*
>
> ***When he reached Laramie**, he looked for a hotel.*
>
> *I know three people **who live in Boston.***

5.4. Other grammatical terms A-Z

Active: In English, most statements are made using the **active** voice. In an active statement, the **subject** is the doer of the action expressed by means of the verb. For example *The students were studying English*.

Apposition: Normally a direct sequence of two nouns, with no intervening preposition, which <u>both refer to the same entity</u>:

> Examples: *President Eisesnhower / The car, a Tesla ...*
>
> *The painting, a work by Rembrandt,....*

In English, except in titles (such as *Doctor Jekyll*), the second or "apposed" noun requires a determiner, normally an article. Apposition should not be confused with compound nouns, in which two nouns placed next to each other refer to different things; for example *The shop window*

Aspect: In English, verbs can be expressed in two aspects, the **simple** aspect (such as *I drink*) or the **progressive** aspect (such as *I am drinking*).

Attributive: An adjective that is **attributive** is one that is placed in front of the noun it qualifies (as in *A good book*).Contrast with adjectives following a copular verb such as *be* , which are called predicative adjectives (as in *This book is good*).

Auxiliary: A verb that comes before a main verb to designate a tense, a modality or the passive voice. The basic auxiliaries are *be* and *have*: modal auxiliaries are *will, shall, may, might, must, can, be able to* and their other forms.

Catenative verbs or **consecutive verbs**. Verbs that can be followed directly by a second verb, with no intervening noun or pronoun (as in *I like playing football*). See *Consecutive verbs.*

Communication: The object of speech or writing. Communication cannot be successful unless the **producer** (speaker, writer) and the **receiver** (listener, reader) are using the same language **code**. The code consists of two elements: vocabulary (words) and grammar (how those words are organised).

Comparative: A particular meaning that is given to an adjective or adverb either by adding *-er* to the end of an adjective, or by adding *more* before an adjective or adverb.

Complement:: The main element of the predicate after a copular verb. See *object* above, see *copular verb* below.

Conjunctive adverb: A type of **connector**, a type of *sentence adverb* used to express a particular relationship between a first clause and a second clause that follows. Examples: *Therefore, however, similarly.*   See *Conjunctive adverbs (§ 3.4)*

Connector: A word that links two similar items (words, phrases, clauses). Connectors are either conjunctions or conjunctive adverbs. See conjunctions

Coordination: Linking two or more elements with similar status in the sentence.

Copular verb: A verb whose complement is not an object, but a description of the subject. Examples: *The car is red, I feel sick, The children became very excited.*

Declarative: A declarative sentence is a normal sentence, which is neither an interrogative sentence (question), nor an exclamation, nor an imperative. A declarative sentence can be affirmative or negative.

Examples: *The man is sitting on a chair,* and *The man is not sitting on a chair* are both declarative statements.

Determiner: **Determiners** are used at the start of a noun phrase. The most common determiners are articles; but determiners also include demonstratives, numerals, or possessive determiners. All nouns or noun phrases require a determiner unless they are used as generalisations.

> Examples: *The man is eating his dinner*, and *That man is eating fries.*

No determiner is required before *fries*, which is used as a generalisation. For more on this, see count and non-count nouns.

Discourse marker: A word or phrase, usually a conjunctive adverb, a filler or a free-standing adverb, which indicates the relation of one sentence or phrase to the next.

Ellipsis: A statement that is reduced to a minimum number of words, by the elimination of words whose meaning can be implied or inferred. For example *the man in the garden* can be understood as an ellipsis of *the man who is in the garden*. Or the simple expression *London* can exist as an **elliptical** sentence in reply to the question *Where do you live?* — the elliptical sentence implying the meaning *I live in Washington*.

Endings: Also called suffixes, endings are grammatical or functional morphemes that are added to the end of word to inflect or change its meaning. Compared to many languages, English has relatively few endings. There are actually only three common endings in English that are used to make inflected forms of a word, without changing its category. These are *-ing, -ed,* and *-s* for verbs, and *-s* for nouns. Other endings are used to change the grammatical category of a word, for example *-ness* or *-ity* that form nouns from adjectives, or *-ful or -less* that form adjectives from nouns.

Gerund: A Gerund is a type of *-ing word*. To distinguish gerunds from present participles, *see* *§ 1.9 Gerunds.*

Gradable: Adjectives are called **gradable** if they can be modified by an **intensifier** such as *very, quite or extremely*. Most adjectives are gradable, but some are not. For example we can say *A rather expensive car* or *The children became very excited*, but we cannot say *John has a very electric car*. A car is electric, or it is not electric. It cannot be *very electric*, or *quite electric*.

Grammar: The corpus of rules and principles that describe how a language is used or should be used. Grammar can be **prescriptive** (telling people what is correct and what is not) , or **descriptive**

(describing what how people actually use language). Grammar is constantly evolving, but it does so more slowly that vocabulary. As well as traditional grammar, linguists have developed other types of grammar to better analyse language, such as transformational grammar or generative grammar.

Imperative: The form of the verb that we use when we give an order or a command. See Imperative.

Indicative: In English, almost all verbs are used in the indicative mood. The subjunctive, the other principal mood, is rare.

Intensifier: A type of adverb that is used to give extra force to the meaning of an adjective. Examples: *very / extremely / most / highly*

Metalanguage: In linguistics, the words and expressions used to describe language itself. The expressions explained on this page are the essential terms used to describe language in English.

Modal verb: Modal verbs, or modal auxiliaries, such as *can* or *must*, are used to express possibility, obligation, probability or futurity. See § 1.15 Modals of obligation, *§ 1.16 Modals of possibility* , *§ 1.3 Expressing the future.*

Modify: In grammar, the word *modify* most commonly means to give a specific meaning to a noun or verb. Modifiers include adjectives, adverbs and prepositional phrases

Mood: In English there are three moods, the **indicative,** the **subjunctive** and the **indicative**. The subjunctive is very rarely used.

Passive: A passive sentence is one in which the subject is the topic of the action, not the actor or agent. See *§ 1.8 The passive voice.*

Example: *The tree was blown over by the wind.* In this example, the actor or agent of the action is *the wind.*

Predicate: One of the two essential constituents of a sentence, the other one being the **subject**. The predicate is made up of everything in the sentence that is not contained in the subject. In a normal affirmative sentence, it follows the subject. It must contain a verb.

Punctuation: An aspect of syntax, punctuation consists of a small number of symbols that are used to delimit, when necessary, words, phrases or sentences. See § 4.7 Punctuation

Quantifier: A quantifier is a type of **determiner** that expresses an imprecise or undefined quantity; it can be contrasted with a number that expresses a precise quantity. Quantifiers include words such as *some, many, a few, several*. See § *2.6. Quantifiers*

Relative: A relative clause is a clause introduced by a relative pronoun such as *who, which, whose* etc.

Subject: The actor or topic of a sentence. In a simple sentence, the subject comes first, before the predicate.

Subordination: see *subordinate clause* above.

Suffix: A morpheme (element of meaning) added to the end of a word. See *endings* above.

Style: The manner in which ideas are expressed as words. Style can be anything from formal to informal, or oral to written. See § *4.9. Style in English.*

Superlative: The highest degree of an adjective or adverb. Superlatives are formed either by adding *-est* to an adjective, or by adding the word *most* before an adjective or an adverb.

Syllable: In phonetics, a unit of sound. Some words are monosyllables, with just one unit of sound, for example *I, egg, boy, this, stand*; other words are made up of two or more syllables, for example *nation, basket, given, complicated.*

Syntax: An aspect of grammar, syntax deals with the way in which words are organized and ordered. It includes word order and punctuation.

Tense: Tenses are specific forms of verbs which are used to situate an action in time. According to a current convention in modern linguistics, English just has two tenses, the present tense and the past tense; but this is just one way of classifying tenses in English, and not necessarily the most logical way.

> For purposes of simplicity and clarity, many books and language teachers use the word tense in a much broader sense, to describe each of the different forms of a verb used to denote a different time frame – as is accepted practice for languages like French Spanish or Russian.

> It is important to understand that there is no absolute truth. Saying that there are two tenses in English is not any more accurate, nor more exact, than saying there are six tenses, or even twelve tenses, as many eminent grammarians have done in the past. It depends on the criteria used to define the notion of "tense".

English verbs come in different forms and different aspects, so for example in the two-tense model, the English present **tense** is a single tense with four **forms**, the present simple and the present progressive, the present perfect simple and the present perfect progressive. In the six-tense model, these are six different tenses, each with two aspects; and in the twelve-tense model, there are twelve tenses.

Transitive: Verbs are either **transitive** or **intransitive**. Some verbs are always one or the other, some verbs can be either depending on their use. A transitive verb is a verb that must have a direct object.

Example: *The dog was barking / The dog was eating a bone*

In the first example, *barking* is intransitive. It cannot take an object. In the second example, *eating* is used transitively, because there is an object *bone*. The verb *eat* can also be used intransitively, i.e. with no object, as in: *The dog was eating.*

Voice: A key factor describing the way in which a verb is used. There are two voices, the **active** and the **passive**.   See *verbs.*

Appendix

Alphabetical list of 80 common consecutive verbs

- Note that apart from **allow**, used as an example, the table below does not include ► verbs of authority (permit, forbid, let), modal verbs, or non-consecutive verbs.

In this table, each verb is listed in the form of a short and realistic example.

Verb, in sample form	Type	followed by a gerund (-ing).	followed by an infinitive with to	Notes
He admitted		doing it *or* <u>to</u> doing it		
He advised	1	taking the train.	us to take the train	Depends on the structure
I can afford	1	(rare)	to buy a new car	Gerund sometimes used in negative structures
I agreed	1		to meet him at 8.	
I aim	1		to finish on time	
I **allow**	1		you to go home now.	Can only be used consecutively in the passive
I appreciate	2	being here.		
I arranged	1		to meet him.	
She asked	1		to go home.	
She attempted	1		to hide.	
I avoid	2	traveling on busy days		
I can't bear	2	living in New York	to be without you.	Slightly different meanings.
He begged	1		to stay.	
I begin		(rare in present)	to understand.	
He didn't bother		telling anyone	to tell anyone.	Either structure possible
I choose	1		to remain silent.	
She completed		filling in the form.		
She consented			to marry him.	
She considered		going to South Africa.		
He continued	2	living in Chicago	to live in Chicago.	The same meaning.
But!! He	2	living in Chicago	to live in Chicago.	Take care! Two

went on				different meanings
He dares	1		to argue with me.	or: argue with me.
He decided	1		to stop smoking.	
I delayed		going to New York.		
To deny		having been present.		
He deserves	1		to be punished.	
I detest	2	eating fish.		
I dislike	2	eating fish.		
I enjoy	2	eating fish.		
I expect	1		to win first prize.	
He failed			to win a prize.	
He finished		building the wall.		
She forget			to say she was going home.	
I am going	1	swimming.	to swim.	Take care! Slightly different meanings
He happened			to hear her.	
He helped			to paint the garage.	Take care! Also ..paint the garage.
I couldn't help		hearing what you said.		Take care!
I hesitate	1		to do that.	
I hope	1		to be there	
He imagined	2	living in Tahiti.		
I intend	1		to be there.	
He will learn			to speak English	
I like or love	2	being with you	to be with you	Either structure possible
But!! I would like	2	living in L.A.	to live in L.A..	Take care! Slightly different meanings
I long	1		to be with you.	
It means	2	starting again.		Take care! in the sense of implies
He means	1		to start again	Take care! in the sense of plans
I don't mind	2	living in Chicago.		
I miss	2	seeing you.		
He neglected			to say he was going out.	

He offered	1		to help	
I plan	1	being here by 8.	to be here by 8.	The gerund form is not common
She practiced		singing all day.		
I prefer	2	living here	to take the plane.	
They prepared	1		to welcome the President.	
I pretended			to laugh.	
She proceeded (went on)	1		to win the match.	
I promise	1		to be good.	
I propose	1	staying here	to go home.	Depends on the context.
I recall		living in London.		
I recommend		seeing this movie	<u>you</u> to see this movie	Depends on the context.
He refused	1		to change his mind.	
I remembered		living in London.	to shut the door.	Take care! Different meanings.
I regret	2	having done that.		
I resumed		reading my book.		
She risked		being seen.		
It seems			to be OK.	
I can't stand	2	eating zucchini.		
I started		reading.	to read.	Either structure possible
I stopped		reading.	to have a drink.	Take care! Two different meanings
I suggest		going home now.		
I swear	1		to tell the truth.	
I tend			to agree with you.	
He threatened	1		to hit me.	
Will you try		opening this for me!	to open it?	Slightly different meanings
He undertakes	1		to finish it by midnight.	
I'm waiting	1		to go home.	
I want	2	to go home.		
I wish	2	to go home.		

9 791069 977631